MW01228801

Prescription for Healthy Relationships

A Practical Guide to Overcoming Offences

Valentine A. Rodney

For Conferences, Workshop, Crusades, Conventions and Seminars contact: Rev. Valentine Rodney
c/o Word Impact Ministries International
P.O. Box 787
Spanish Town
St. Catherine
Jamaica

Email: varodney@gmail.com

Tel: Jamaica: 876 390 2303 | USA: 407 545 5052

Published by:

Book Cover Design by: Iconence (www.iconence.com)

ISBN: 978-1-958404-36-2 (paperback)
978-1-958404-37-9 (hardback)

First Edition: March 2023

Scripture quotations marked (NLT) are taken from the Holy Bible, New Living Translation, copyright © 1996, 2004, 2007 by Tyndale House Foundation. Used by permission of Tyndale House Publishers, Inc., Carol Stream, Illinois 60188. All rights reserved.

Dedication

This book is dedicated to the multitudes of those affected by the tragedy of offence, which includes both the victims and the perpetrators.

In a real way, both the offended and the offender are victims of this cruel state of affair. It is my hope that as the lifeline is being extended, many will be pulled to the harbour of safety where healing, restoration, and recovery will move them from being victims to victorious living.

Acknowledgment

The author wishes to acknowledge the real Hero who inspired this writing, and who has been my lifelong coach and confidant, the Lord Jesus Christ. His providential guidance has been instrumental in providing a pathway of restoration and recovery to deal with this continued, existing threat to harmonious relationships.

That healing from offences is possible is strongly articulated in the manual we call the scriptures (Bible). The Word of God provides both curative and preventative ways of dealing with this age-old problem to healthy and balanced interpersonal relationships.

I wish to also thank my collaborators, Dr. Carla Dunbar, Minister Megan Hylton, Rev. Denise Hinkson-Lawrence, and Rev. Nicholas Robertson for the interaction and their invaluable insights and contribution in writing their respective chapters.

I wish to also pay my regards to all those who gave written endorsements, and to Cay Maria Boswell for the forward.

What can I say about my publisher, Author C. Orville McLeish, who laid the foundation and really kickstarted and continues to support me as an author. I still recall how he would not quit talking to me until the first manuscript was written, which gave me the boost and confidence to encourage and edify thousands of readers.

To all those who believed in and supported me, I show my sincere gratitude by continuing to teach, preach and model a lifestyle consistent with my Christian convictions and beliefs.

To my wife, Yevett, and daughters, Zharia and Ana-Olivia, thanks for bearing with me and being my biggest supporters.

Endorsements

This is a balanced approach to dealing with this most vexing issue affecting human relationships at all levels, and shaking the foundations of institutions, the church not exempted. Valentine interacts with the biblical text and human experience to help us avoid and navigate what he calls the brutality of offence.

This book is a helpful tool for equipping those who are called to mediate and provide help and healing to both offender and offended.

Bishop Wantworth B. Heron

Pastor

Lehigh Acres Church of God of Prophecy

I have read many books pertaining to the effects of a damaged soul, but this book was different as it is rooted in the Word of God from cover to cover. I have not seen a more satisfying, Bible-based, and succinctly written book on how to deal with toxic emotions.

Finally, someone is not just focusing on telling the believers to go pray and fast but rather how to recognize the toxicity and how to deal with them. This book is not just for those who have experienced offences, but also for the offenders.

Reverend Valentine Rodney enters the lives of those who have been affected by offences and with humility and respect addresses their pain with balance and provides resources geared towards dealing with offences from a Christian perspective. This book provides a most refreshing approach to the subject of forgiveness and right relationship with others.

As a counsellor, I find this book to be useful for couples counselling, trauma counselling, sexual abuse counselling, domestic abuse counselling, interpersonal communication problems, and some personality issues that many struggle with within the church setting and other relationships. I believe this book can be used by any counsellor—Christian or non-Christian—because of the author's emphasis on the special ways to help deal with the inevitability of offences.

The tools given are written from a Biblical framework that I call "theocentric" interventions but is also applicable in any therapeutic setting that fosters forgiveness as a therapeutic intervention. Additionally, there are powerful insights in the chapter "Offence in Marriage" that arises due to lack of understanding which sets a framework that is very thoughtful and biblically astute.

I believe that every pastor and counsellor, especially those who specialize in marriage counselling, should get this book. This chapter brought some great insights to me personally, so I believe this chapter could give any marriage counsellor some new ways of helping couples to navigate through those very challenging issues.

Finally, Reverend Valentine Rodney has demonstrated a genuine understanding of the impact of offences on the soul of individuals, and the healing process that is necessary to bring them back into congruency with others and with God. What this book says about human nature when it comes to offences and the Godly way of dealing with them gives me, the counsellor, some new insights for myself, as well as for my clients.

I must say this is an excellent book that every Christian counsellor and pastor should read. Rev. Rodney has incorporated a sound theological framework into a comprehensive deliverance approach for the offended and the offenders. He presents a well-balanced perspective on current controversial and relational issues that all Christian counsellors and pastors can utilize.

I endorse this book, and it will be a part of my counselling toolbox.

Paula Haughton-Keen

Clinical Mental Health Counsellor

Master of Arts of Clinical Mental Health Counselling
Member of the American Counselling Association

Rev. Valentine Rodney could not have chosen a better time to present this valuable resource to a world that is now dominated by the era of offence that is found everywhere, in our homes, marriages, relationships, friendships, workplaces, churches, and society at large. The book "Prescription for Healthy Relationships: A Practical Guide to Overcoming Offences," provides pragmatic solutions that will help in dealing with the matter of offences. It is the author's objective that this book will be a catalyst for change and will have a profound impact on the way offences are dealt with in our daily lives.

If you want to experience lasting and meaningful relationships, I highly recommend this book as a must-have.

Get your copy today!

Nadine G. Reid, MBA., BSc.,
Author
Host of Your Inspiration Connection Podcast

Personal, compelling, and practical, Rev. Valentine Rodney helps you grasp the psychology of offence and how to protect your mental health against the cancel culture. He shares practical tools and strategies on how to face and feel the offence. Failing to feel the offence results in carrying false guilt.

Rev. Rodney shares insights on interpersonal offence, hypersensitivity, and its profound effects on one's mental well-being. Past embedded emotions can be a trigger in our present relationships. Rev. Rodney did not shy away from addressing this element of offence in marriages. Mishandling an offence, or trying to manage it, can lead to more conflict, bitterness, and mental illness. It can ruin your relationships on many levels. Did you know you can protect your heart from bitterness, and the sting of offence? Learn the biblical truths and practical "how to" in this book.

This is an overall excellent and must-read book.

Rev. Denise Hinkson Lawrence

Owner of Women 2 Women LLC
Life Coach, Author, Podcaster, Speaker, and Host

"When someone gives you offence, it doesn't mean you have to take it." ~ Joyce Meyer.

Being a pastor for over twenty-three years and a marriage officer for over ten years, I can say from experience that the information given within this book by Rev. Valentine Rodney about offence is well-researched, organised and well presented. I love the varied perspectives he writes from, speaking about the victim and the victimiser. The information presented is relevant, so each reader can identify with it.

I also love the fact that the intended audience goes far beyond the Christian community, as this book is generally quite applicable to companies, organisations, and families. I know without a doubt that reading this first volume will bring a strong desire for volume two. It would be remiss of me not to mention the carefully detailed "Prescription for a Better You" given by Rev. Rodney, which puts the icing on the cake for a more fulfilled life as we deal with the various offences we face daily.

Bishop Dr. Pete Pinnock

Calvary Evangelistic Assembly

John Maxwell Certified, Speaker, Trainer & Coach

In his latest book, Rev. Valentine Rodney gives clear and precise teaching on the topic of offence that is grounded in biblical truth. He points readers to practical examples of offence from scripture, offers insightful teaching on how to handle offence however it presents itself in our daily lives and offers tips for dealing with this most common issue.

I like the fact that the author places a special focus on offence in marriage and offers readers guidance on how to deal with the touchy issues that might cause conflicts between spouses. By focusing on communication styles, couples can receive practical guidance on how to improve this essential aspect of their relationship so as not to repeat offences.

The questions at the end are the icing on top of the cake. The reader is not left on their own to figure out how they can apply the wisdom in the chapters since the author asks probing, useful questions to help readers apply the knowledge gained from this book. I think everyone should read this book, singles and couples alike. It is an invaluable tool in these trying times.

A must read!

Dwania Duhaney-Millen

Dip. English (hons), B.Ed. English (hons), M.A. English (dist.)

Educator, Blogger, Author: Not a Single Shade of Grey

About the Author

REV. VALENTINE A. RODNEY, BSc, MA. is an international speaker whose ministry has taken him to the USA, Canada, Europe, Africa, and several countries within the Caribbean, where he has also fostered and facilitated ministerial developmental programmes. He has done undergraduate work at the University of the West Indies in Marine Biology and Graduate work in Missions at the Caribbean Graduate School of Theology.

Rev. Rodney has served in the areas of Christian Education, Evangelism, Leadership Development, Prayer and Intercession, Youth Ministry, Radio and Television and Pastorate. He is also actively involved in welfare Programmes and mentorship to men, youths, and ministers. He is a strong advocate for Christian Transformational Development where the church interfaces with the community and assists in strategic intervention that is both redemptive and empowering.

He is the Author of the Books: Shameless Persistence - The Audacity of Purposeful Praying, A Way of Escape - How to

Handle the Tests and Temptations of Life, The Power of the Secret Place - The Place of Relationship, Resolution and Revelation, and La Persistencia Desvergonzada: La audacia de la oración con propósito. He has co-authored seven other books with his friend and ministerial colleague, Rev. Nicholas "Robdon" Robertson. Rev. Rodney is the host and presenter of the television programme *Word Impact* aired on MTM tv.

Rev. Rodney is an International Instructor for Walk Thru the Bible Ministries, Co-Founder and Deputy Director for Impact Online Bible Institute (IOBI), Deputy Director of Build A Man Foundation and the Director of Word Impact Ministries International, a non-denominational ministry that caters to the empowerment of the Christian Community and the salvation of the lost.

He is an International Chaplain and Ambassador with Covenant International University and Seminary. His Motto is *"Go Where There Is No Path and Leave a Trail."*

VALENTINE A. RODNEY is married to Yevett for over twenty-six years. Their union has produced two daughters, Zharia and Ana-Olivia.

Foreword

Our lives are cycles of interactions where we are either actively engaged in giving of ourselves or receiving from others. As a leader, educator, daughter, sister, friend, and colleague, I fulfil many roles on a daily basis that allow me to engage in multiple interactions with different people. These interactions may open the door for me to be the recipient or deliverer of offence. The light in this cycle, however, is that whether we give or receive, there is hope for reconciling us back to ourselves and others and, ultimately, back to our Father.

Valentine A. Rodney, or Uncle Rodney and Rev. Rodney, as I have called him for over twenty-five years, continues to engage us in the reflective work of self-examination through prayer (Shameless Persistence) and the secret place (The Power of the Secret Place) in order to find the ways of escape (A Way of Escape) from the spiritual hazards that we encounter in our walk with God and our fellow humans. Rev. Rodney has encapsulated the importance of the process of reconciliation and healing for both the offender and the offended in the pages that follow. He emphasizes what God expects of us as we pursue Him in our daily lives and strive to live His commandment to love each other as we love ourselves and Christ.

With Prescription for Healthy Relationships: A Practical Guide to Overcoming Offences, Rev. Rodney has penned practical steps and strategies for us to embrace and practice in order to live victoriously in our relationships as God promised us while we sojourn here. As you read the words on the pages, you will be led by the Holy Spirit into places of power with relationships founded upon love and obedience, while overcoming our desires to be right. The words on these pages will encourage you to seek peace and pursue it both within your own heart and in your relationships with others.

Like a true spiritual apothecary, Rev. Rodney has skilfully captured the specific content for healing ourselves and our relationships when the disease of offence is the diagnosis. These strategies have been interwoven with scripture and expertly presented for immediate application in our daily living. I pray that as you read these words, your application of its prescription will lead to a renewal of your mind and relationships that bring you to living Jesus' prayer in John 17:21: *"I pray that they will all be one, just as you and I are one—as you are in me, Father, and I am in you. And may they be in us so that the world will believe you sent me." (NLT).*

Cay Maria Boswell, BA, GradCert, M.Sc., AC

Assistant Principal/Educator

Bronx New York

Table of Contents

Introduction

The issue of offence, whether the giving or receiving of it, is a considerable threat and a major problem when considering the dynamics of interpersonal relationships. It has contributed in many ways to the breakdown in communications and caused many to feel emotionally and mentally drained, frustrated, hurt, and distanced. The feelings caused by offences not only puts a strain on interpersonal relationships but also affects the reputation and self-esteem of the offended.

We are going to consider throughout this volume, offence, the offended and the offender. An evaluation of all three will be critical not just to understanding but the presenting of useful strategies to provide help and healing.

In dealing with offences, one can either react or respond. The knee-jerk reaction exhibited by some is symptomatic of both defensive and offensive coping mechanisms. While we can put offences in broad categories and summarily predict what may be the ensuing responses, it is true to say that the responses are highly subjective and wholly dependent on the individual. Several underlying factors may have an overall effect on whether the individual becomes retaliatory or simply acquiesces into silence as they internalise the emotional pain being experienced.

Much damage has resulted from offences and sometimes not even time provides the healing sought. Without specific intervention strategies, many will never be able to overcome and live a "normal life."

Jesus, the master teacher, in Luke 17:1, gave us a fitting reminder, *"Then said he unto the disciples, it is impossible but that offences will come: but woe unto him, through whom they come!" (KJV).* Like death and taxes, offences are unavoidable. They will happen whether you are prepared, unprepared, or underprepared. In many instances, it is virtually impossible to avoid either being offended or becoming the offender. The thought reflected here by Jesus is that situations will naturally arise where the giving or receiving of offences will take place.

There will be major questions, for example, Why does it hurt so bad? Why am I so vulnerable? Why do I keep hurting others? These are among the myriad of thoughts that may plague the mind of both the offender and the offended.

In many instances, the one hurt, rather than dealing with the situation, tends to distance themselves from the source of the pain or keep excusing the offender. Either of these options is a recipe for disaster. You cannot conquer what you fail to confront. The confrontations need to be done on both levels. The offended needs to confront the offender and the offender needs to confront themselves, the purpose of the confrontation being geared towards reconciliation. It is going to require honesty and determination from both to see the process through.

Individually, there needs to be some introspection to determine what causes one to react or respond in a particular manner to potentially offensive situations. This should be with the view of submitting to a process of healing once the trigger has been identified. There are times when the help that is needed will have to come through submitting to the intervention of a skilled helper (counsellor). Sometimes you must revisit the past to change the future. Self-medicating can help, while in other cases, it must be administered.

The cause of offence may be deliberate or unintentional, but that does not lessen the pain caused and the need for proper resolution.

The intention of this author is to use the scriptures and other source materials as a guide to look at the causes, categories, effects, and the treatment of offences. Consideration will be given to providing an effective guide to resolution. The worldview of the offender and the offended will be examined so that both can receive the help that is most needed.

One volume is certainly not expansive enough to address all the aspects of offence, but this volume is expected to begin for some and continue for others the conversation in the hope that some will receive help and others will shoulder the responsibility of providing useful insights into dealing with such a critical subject matter. There is too much at stake to allow this cancer to continue to wreak havoc. It must be identified, cauterised, and dealt with urgently.

The brutality of offence lies in its ability to convict the convicted, abuse the abused, and incarcerate the victim, but both the offender and offended party are victims of this unwelcome but obtrusive enemy of relationships. It is also possible that the offended can become the offender and the offender become offended. In this case, the tables are turned but the hurt continues as no one has been healed from the trauma. Offence can be both motivating and demotivating. It can inspire and motivate one to deal with their own issues of vulnerability and become strengthened in conflict resolution or simply become so crushed and distraught that a cycle of dysfunctionality is perpetuated.

As you interact with the material, take time to pause and reflect. It is the author's expectation that the material presented may challenge you to change whether you are a victim or a victimiser. The intent however is quite clear that we need to, in some way or the other, reduce the cycle of hurts by appropriate interventions. It is better to prevent than to seek for a cure.

Chapter 1

Offences Will Come

An honest man speaks the truth, though it may give offence; a vain man, in order that it may. —William Hazitt

Then said he unto the disciples, It is impossible but that offences will come: but woe unto him, through whom they come! It were better for him that a millstone were hanged about his neck, and he cast into the sea, than that he should offend one of these little ones. Take heed to yourselves: If thy brother trespass against thee, rebuke him; and if he repent, forgive him. And if he trespass against thee seven times in a day, and seven times in a day turn again to thee, saying, I repent; thou shalt forgive him. And the apostles said unto the Lord, Increase our faith. (*Luke 17:1-5*).

Jesus underscores the point that if you are human, you can never completely avoid situations or people that cause offence. We should not be surprised when this happens. It is simply one of the highly regrettable hazards of interpersonal relationships.

Offences are inevitable being based on the corruption of human nature through the fall, the snares of the world and the temptations of Satan. Despite our best efforts, offences will be given and taken. Even those professing to follow Jesus will either stumble and be hindered or themselves put an occasion in the way of others to stumble.

There is however a fundamental difference between finding something offensive and being offended by it. The choices that we make determines how we are affected or influenced. A situation may be deemed offensive, but you consciously decide not to be offended by it. Allowing yourself to be open to or victimised by offence gives rise to the offender influencing your emotional well-being and, subsequently, your behavioural pattern. This may result in you becoming open to abuse and manipulation. Let us therefore maintain and preserve what influences our heart.

Guard your heart above all else, for it determines the course of your life. (Proverbs 4:23 - NLT).

The Merriam Webster Dictionary states that offence is *"something that outrages the moral or physical senses, the act of displeasing or affronting, a breach of a moral or social code and a cause or occasion to sin."* It is evident that what causes offence is identifiable and the effects are pronounced whether the action is deliberate or unintentional.

The Oxford Dictionary states that as a noun, offence means *"annoyance or resentment brought about by a perceived insult or disregard of oneself, a thing that constitutes a violation of what is judged to be right or natural and the action of attacking someone or something."*

Offence in this passage (see Luke 17:1-5) comes from the Greek word *skandalon,* which means a trap spring, a stick for the bait of a trap, a snare, or a stumbling block. The trigger of a trap (the mechanism closing a trap down on the unsuspecting victim), (figuratively) putting a negative cause-and-effect relationship into motion. The means of stumbling; this stresses the method (means) of entrapment (caught by your own devices like personal bias or carnal thinking). Native rock rising up through the earth that trips a traveller (used of Jesus, especially to the Jews who refused to believe in Him).

The hurt to the offended and the consequences to the offender are clearly outlined by the passage (see Luke 17:1-5). There is a strong penalty to be imposed upon those who are the causative agents of offence.

In the Bible, sometimes a *skandalon* is good, referring to the way people "trip" over Jesus and are offended at the gospel. It is figuratively applied to Jesus Christ, whose person and career were so contrary to the expectations of the Jews concerning the Messiah, that they rejected Him, and by their obstinacy made shipwreck of their salvation.

God warned them of this in the Scriptures when He said, "I am placing a stone in Jerusalem that makes people stumble, a rock that makes them fall. But anyone who trusts in him will never be disgraced." (Romans 9:33 - NLT).

Dear brothers and sisters, if I were still preaching that you must be circumcised—as some say I do—why am I still being persecuted? If I were no longer preaching salvation through the cross of Christ, no one would be offended. (Galatians 5:11 - NLT).

However, a *skandalon* among believers is seen as negative. It could refer to false counsel.

Jesus turned to Peter and said, "Get away from me, Satan! You are a dangerous trap to me. You are seeing things merely from a human point of view, not from God's." (Matthew 16:23 - NLT).

You can lead a brother into sin by your "liberty":

So let's stop condemning each other. Decide instead to live in such a way that you will not cause another believer to stumble and fall. (Romans 14:13 - NLT).

Division and false teaching bring a *skandalon* among God's people.

And now I make one more appeal, my dear brothers and sisters. Watch out for people who cause divisions and upset people's faith by teaching things contrary to what you have been taught. Stay away from them. (Romans 16:17 - NLT).

The bait to offend will be offered, but woe to the one who offers the hook. In other words, people will take the bait but woe to the one who provides a reason to stumble in the way of others. The judgment and punishment against offending, as stated by Jesus, is severe, clearly demonstrating how serious this action is viewed by God. This is particularly so when one considers that rather than guiding and covering, the offence causes the recent converts to turn from following Christ. Offending can be both mentally and emotionally crushing. God does not require us to function as an instrument of His judgment but rather that of His love. This calls for great introspection and careful analysis of our actions. We must not act without showing due care and consideration to others.

If we show love to each other, we will not bring an offence into the lives of others.

Anyone who loves a fellow believer is living in the light and does not cause others to stumble. (1 John 2:10 - NLT).

John Bevere refers to offence as the Bait of Satan. The bait is used to lure and entice the unsuspecting victim into a trap. Once trapped, the victim is subject to the intent of the trapper.

Attitude Towards Those Who Stumble

It is important that we do not allow ourselves to be victimised and stumble by the conduct and attitudes of others. The need for caution here is being implored by Jesus to avoid the pitfalls. We must also be cautious and not give anyone a reason to fall into sin because of our actions.

We should never pretend that it never happened when someone sins against us. The behaviour should never be ignored but the person must be corrected with love being the guiding principle. When we walk in love with each other, then we stop keeping a record of offences committed against us. The longsuffering nature of the fruit of the Spirit will cause us to adequately deal with the slights and petty offences that we face daily.

Always be humble and gentle. Be patient with each other, making allowance for each other's faults because of your love. (Ephesians 4:2 - NLT).

We cannot afford to be overly sensitive as we seek to bear with each other. When we are sinned against, there is a particular recourse that must be followed. Speak directly to the person causing the offence rather than bottling it up or sharing it with others. It is important that we seek to resolve the issue with the offending party, this being motivated by the unconditional love we should have for each other.

Jesus remarked that the only option we should pursue when the person who offended us repents is to forgive them. But it is also equally true that even if they never repent, we still extend forgiveness and await God working in their lives to facilitate the restoration of relationship. Jesus was not trying to offer us a reason not to forgive but rather to broaden the scope and reach of our forgiveness.

We must never attempt to judge another person's repentance, even if they have sinned repeatedly against us. We might not think they are sincere, but we are charged with the responsibility of forgiving each time they ask. It is a command by Jesus that we must submit to in the hope that as we forgive, then we restore them. The disciples were quick to acknowledge that to get along with people, great faith was needed to keep forgiving the offending party.

Why Are People Offended?

- Unresolved issues
- Unhealed situations
- Unwholesome thought/thinking
- Rejection
- Anger (strained relationship)
- Jealousy
- Wrong perception
- Bad attitude
- Character flaws
- Insecure (not getting their own way)
- Unforgiveness

What we entertain in our thought life has a way of steering the course and subsequent direction of our lives. Most times the tendency is to focus on the negative aspects of relationships while minimising the positive benefits. What becomes your focus is magnified and defended as a means of maintaining the cycle of hurt and pain caused by offence. We must allow for refocussing as a part of the journey towards becoming whole.

Avoid focusing on those that:

- Used or exploited you.
- Simply did not care.
- Took advantage of you.
- Benefited from your demise.
- Were never encouraging.
- Abandoned you in the time of your pain/struggles.
- Never had the patience to stick with you through your process.
- Never had the patience to endure.
- Never believed in you.
- Never listened to you.
- Never had time for you.
- Got tired of you and your problems.

and forgive us our sins, as we have forgiven those who sin against us. (Matthew 6:12 – NLT).

Jesus was fully aware that in the whole gamut of all levels of relationships, offences would come, so He taught us in the model prayer the importance of forgiveness. He taught both the extending and receiving of forgiveness as the potential cure to deal with offences before it careens out of control. We would be well advised to ask God and others for their forgiveness where we have offended and to forgive others who have offended us. This will make for the greatest prescription for dealing with offences. In doing this, we not only release ourselves as the offended but also release the offender.

Chapter 2

Jesus On Dealing With Offence

"People who wish to be offended will always find some occasion for taking offence." —John Wesley

Jesus, the master Teacher, provided some very useful insights relating to the issue of offence both causative and curative. Whereas situations that lead to offences are unavoidable, our response or reaction need not be dictated by the nature of the events. Causing or being the subject of offences does not in any way mean that recovery or healing is impossible. We can heal from our hurts and be much stronger despite what we have been through.

Offence And Civil Responsibility

Jesus cautioned the disciples concerning the importance of ensuring compliance to their civil responsibilities regarding the payment of taxes. He is clearly outlining that omitting to pay taxes would cause an offence to the authorities. Avoiding unnecessary confrontation between state and the believers is alluded to here. There are occasions however where civil disobedience is justifiable because a principle of

God is being violated. This was evident in the Hebrew young men's unwillingness to conform to the decree of the king and societal expectations to bow down and worship the image that Nebuchadnezzar had set up.

"However, we don't want to offend them, so go down to the lake and throw in a line. Open the mouth of the first fish you catch, and you will find a large silver coin. Take it and pay the tax for both of us." (Matthew 17:27 – NLT).

Jesus is advocating compliance with regards to their civil responsibilities. Not everything that is deemed secular is antichrist. While not endorsing any system of unjust taxation, He encourages the payment of taxes as being a special part of their civil responsibilities. Believers must seek to avoid needless controversies that can be potentially explosive and offensive. Christians today must avoid setting a bad example or sending the wrong signal. There are times when we not only fulfil our duty but go beyond and teach and lead by our actions.

Offence As A Stumbling Block

And if thy right hand offend thee, cut it off, and cast it from thee: for it is profitable for thee that one of thy members should perish, and not that thy whole body should be cast into hell. (Matthew 5:30 - KJV).

Careful analysis of this scripture is necessary to understand its real importance. Jesus is in no way advocating mutilation or dismemberment as a means of dealing with offence. This is a hyperbole suggesting, in an exaggerated manner, how vitally important it is to apply the strictest of treatments or measures to offence.

Offence should never be tolerated or entertained because of its potentially devasting effects on both the offender and offended. The literal interpretation does not even go far enough, because with one limb missing, the other could still cause offence. In fact, even with dismemberment, the desire within the heart may still be there. The need to sacrifice is the point here being stressed. How far are you willing to go to treat with the scourge of offence? The poison of offence is detrimental to the quality of life that the believer has been invited to be a partaker of. It is therefore necessary that in our decision-making process, no matter the extent of the sacrifice or commitment that is required, we must do all that is in our power to deal with offence.

There should be more a surrendering of one's will and desires rather than the punishing of oneself to deal with matters that originate from the heart and may represent a deep-seated dysfunctionality within. You can't keep hurting yourself to heal the hurts you have caused to others. There is a discipline that is indeed required and a commitment that, though strict, is necessary.

Offence In The End Times

And then shall many be offended, and shall betray one another, and shall hate one another. (Matthew 24:10 - KJV). With the world increasingly becoming an unstable and unsafe environment, the Bible does provide useful insights into the behaviour of man. One of the characteristics highlighted has to do with interpersonal relationships. Persecution and hardships have a way of revealing the traitors within the believing community and the enemies without.

Jesus knew that after His departure that believers would stumble at the truth, the slowness experienced in obtaining victory and the delays in His second coming. The frustration and discouragement experienced would cause apostasy because of the hostilities being faced. The beatings, imprisonments, deaths, and forcible evacuations because of their faith in Jesus would cause many to stumble and turn away from the faith.

It is easy to be firmly fixed in one's faith when things are tolerably quiet and easy and to shrink back or fall away when the pressures rise based on one's association with Christ. Christ further highlighted that many who once claimed to follow Christ will wane in their commitment to follow Him being unwilling to pay the high cost. There will also be others who, to escape the persecution, will turn traitor to their former friends. They will act out of spite or hate to preserve their own lives.

The end times will see many who followed Christ stumble because they are unwilling to bear with the offence associated with the cross and following Jesus.

Familiarity And Offence

Then they scoffed, "He's just a carpenter, the son of Mary and the brother of James, Joseph, Judas, and Simon. And his sisters live right here among us." They were deeply offended and refused to believe in him. (Mark 6:3 - NLT).

No matter how perfect you are, there will always be persons who are disturbed by what you say and how you represent your ideals. Many will be willing to embrace you and be comfortable provided you do not excel beyond their level of genius. Jesus' return to His hometown Nazareth was not a particularly welcoming one. They spoke disparagingly about Him being a carpenter's son and obviously not having the requisite training in scriptures to be able to teach them. Calling Him the son of Mary was also another way of insulting Jesus. Rumours abounded concerning His illegitimacy and may have occasioned the referencing. Familiarity has a way of breeding both suspicion and contempt.

Past knowledge can become a great barrier to future acceptance. People may be offended not just by what you say but who they perceive you to be. Rather than commending, they found a way to reject and disapprove. They had insufficient information about Him to operate like they knew everything about Him. Familiarity can both prejudice the mind and block receptivity to the truth being presented.

The Word And Offence

But he that received the seed into stony places, the same is he that heareth the word, and anon with joy receiveth it; Yet hath he not root in himself, but dureth for a while: for when tribulation or persecution ariseth because of the word, by and by he is offended. (Matthew 13:20-21 - KJV).

In the above-mentioned parable of Jesus categorised as the Parable of the Sower, the heart is referred to as the stony places. The word is initially received enthusiastically but the effect is short-lived because of an unwillingness to endure the pressures of tribulation or persecution because of the word. It was not the sudden explosive growth that was the source of the problem but rather the lack of depth. This depth is associated with spiritual strength that comes through the Word of God and prayer. Tribulation is the general suffering from outside due to the circumstances of life, whereas persecution takes on a religious motive and is normally deliberately inflicted.

Exposure to reproach and infamy has a way of revealing the hearts of those who profess faith in Christ. Offence will come because there is no strength of principle/character to resist the tests and temptations. The offence taken hardens the heart and affects further growth and development. The offended therefore cannot sustain what they have received, and the word has little or no effect. Offence is said to be like an automatic weapon; once you pull the trigger it keeps on firing.

The Truth And Offence

Then the disciples came to him and asked, "Do you realize you offended the Pharisees by what you just said?" (Matthew 15:12 - NLT).

The transparency that the truth provides can affect those negatively, especially if it discloses their inner thoughts or affects the very core of their belief system. The religious leaders of the day had a knack for stumbling at the truth that Jesus presented. Whereas Jesus was sensitive to the needs of His audience, being always aware of what every heart needed to hear, He never evaded or avoided speaking the truth for fear of offending.

An official delegation had come from Jerusalem to investigate and assess the words and works of Christ. Their early bewilderment would later change to outrage at His words. The discussion that would later provoke the offence revolved around a question concerning the observance of the traditions of the elders. They were offended initially by Jesus' disciple's inobservance of the rigid, extensive rituals for washing before meals, to which Jesus responded that they were setting man's tradition above the Word of God. Truth must be owned, and duty must be done; and if any be offended, it is their own fault. In this regard, offence is not given but taken.

Jesus countered by indicating that the religionists were breaking God's law to maintain their tradition. The keeping of tradition while neglecting or ignoring the Word of God was exemplified as the major problem by Jesus. The issue of eating with unwashed hands was more a question of hygiene than doctrine. The real issue of defilement Jesus posited was what came out rather than what went into a man. Jesus was challenging the very basis of their teaching and rule, making it clear that a person's intent means as much as their actions. The truth can appear to be very antagonistic to the popular or prevailing cultural and religious norms, thereby causing or creating offence.

The truth spoken by Jesus that created the offence revealed both their hearts and actions. They broke the law by taking gifts due to their parents, committing it for religious purposes, thereby removing themselves from the obligation of honouring their parents in word and deed. They, by that action, were setting aside God's Word for the sake of their tradition. Jesus also spoke to their hypocrisy of rendering lip service to God without having a worshipful heart; mouths filled with praise but a heart devoid of devotion to God.

The disciples recognised the dire consequences of Jesus offending the religious leaders intentionally and must have wondered if Jesus had fully calculated the risks involved. But, as St. Gregory observes, "If offence arises from the statement of the truth, it is more expedient that offence be permitted to arise than that the truth should be abandoned."

Offence And Faith

Then saith Jesus unto them, All ye shall be offended because of me this night: for it is written, I will smite the shepherd, and the sheep of the flock shall be scattered abroad. (Matthew 26:31 - KJV).

Disappointments happen when expectation does not live up to reality. The sudden twists and turns of life can have an adverse effect on both the mental and emotional stability. It is even worse when what inspired hope fails to deliver, and tragedy ensues.

The disciples were brimming with confidence having found the long-awaited Messiah to which the scriptures referred. Their joy turned to disappointment upon realisation that Jesus did not come to fulfil their ideals of a conquering Messiah but instead a suffering saviour as prefigured in the book of Isaiah. Several times He would allude to the fact that His mission was to die. They could not see at the time the fulfilling of God's purpose. They were looking forward to the overthrowing of Roman domination and the restoration of Israel's theocracy.

Jesus' shocking statement regarding the catastrophic days ahead was enough to send them into a tailspin. He mentioned that all would be offended. Their confidence would be shaken, and trust turned to disbelief. They would stumble in their walk with Him upon witnessing the cruel atrocities that would be committed against Him. It would be difficult for them to absorb and deal with a Messiah that would be victimised at the hands of cruel men. Their faith was centered around a living Christ, and His death cast a dark shadow over everything He had taught for over three years.

Faith can take a serious battering when despite our convictions the opposite to what we are believing God for occurs. They were no longer compelled to continue or pursue the path of following a Jesus that could not or, at best, would not defend Himself. Offence will cause you to walk away and distance yourself from the source of your pain and discomfort. They had invested so much time and energy, and now their dreams were rapidly fading and disintegrating before their very eyes. Offence will drain you of the energy needed to stand and cause you to return to what you were delivered from.

There is nothing like a storm to cause the effects of offence to be displayed. To them, their leader had failed in His mission, and this was far more than they were able to cope with. The ending of a cycle of leadership can create an opportunity for many to stumble and fall away from their earlier convictions.

Offence And Forgiveness

Take heed to yourselves: If thy brother trespass against thee, rebuke him; and if he repent, forgive him. And if he trespass against thee seven times in a day, and seven times in a day turn again to thee, saying, I repent; thou shalt forgive him. And the apostles said unto the Lord, Increase our faith. And the Lord said, If ye had faith as a grain of mustard seed, ye might say unto this sycamine tree, Be thou plucked up by the root, and be thou planted in the sea; and it should obey you. (Luke 17:3-6 – KJV).

Jesus here is emphasising the importance of faith in producing the forgiveness required to release someone that has offended you through transgression. He is quick to point out that we must watch and consider the state of our own hearts. It is possible to be so offended by the actions of others that we move to retaliate and so offend causing another to stumble. The answer is not in playing the victim or becoming the victimiser but simply in reposing such trust and confidence in God that you release the offender through forgiveness when asked and, by extension, even when it is not requested as a true symbol or sign and indeed testimony of your faith in God.

Faith in God is capable of uprooting bitterness and unforgiveness, irrespective of how deeply entrenched or how long it has been rooted. The biblical requirement in dealing with offence is to pardon the offender no matter how challenging the situation is. It is out of our relationship with

God that we can establish so firm a footing that we produce the peaceable fruit of forgiveness because of the root of faith in Him. It is not up to us to question the sincerity of the person requesting forgiveness irrespective of how often they transgress, for it is only God who can discern the intent of the heart.

It is understandable that the deeper the hurt, the more difficult it is to deal with both the pain and the source of our discomfort. A difficult situation should never be equated with an impossible one. Stop failing before trying. Jesus however does not make this optional but rather lays it squarely on our ability to believe and trust. Forgiving does not imply condoning the behaviour but releasing the offender, thereby allowing for an opportunity of both conviction and healing.

The empowering nature of faith in God coupled with His abiding presence will provide for us the ability to step out by faith into forgiveness. For some, this may imply cautious optimism that the offence will not be repeated because it has been challenged. This challenge may require not just a stating of the transgression but a rebuking to facilitate the kind of humility that will result in a repentant heart and the salvation of the offender. It is abundantly clear that exhibiting this kind of faith will require appropriating both love and enduring patience. Time must be given for the work of the Holy Spirit in the heart of the individual. The offended party must try to avoid becoming defensive and mistrustful in all other encounters.

Faith teaches that as we abide in Jesus and His Word in us, then we can ask for a forgiving heart (one that reflects and radiates the fruit of the Spirit) and it will be given to us.

But if you remain in me and my words remain in you, you may ask for anything you want, and it will be granted! When you produce much fruit, you are my true disciples. This brings great glory to my Father. (John 15:7-8 - NLT).

The strength of our abiding relationship with Jesus is borne out by our ability to forgive and be healed from offences. We cannot embrace a loving God and not be concerned about the welfare of His children. Even as we do not want to stumble through the activities of others, we also should not put a cause in someone's way to stumble. Use the opportunity to help rather than hurt and to restore rather than widen the rift.

But I say unto you, That ye resist not evil: but whosoever shall smite thee on thy right cheek, turn to him the other also. (Matthew 5:39 - KJV).

What is alluded to in this text is not to receive physical harm and endangerment without attempting to protect oneself, but rather it stands as a metaphor for being insulted but not resisting within the context of interpersonal relationships. This is often unavoidable.

And the Lord said, If ye had faith as a grain of mustard seed, ye might say unto this sycamine tree, Be thou plucked up by the root, and be thou planted in the sea; and it should obey you. (Luke 17:6 - KJV).

Jesus uses the example of the sycamine tree to show the effects of bitterness and unforgiveness. Just as the Sycamine tree grows quickly, so does bitterness and unforgiveness. Fast-growing ugly attitudes are allowed to grow freely and spoil the condition of the heart. These negative attitudes grow best in dry spiritual conditions and are deadly.

The roots of the sycamine tree are extraordinarily strong and can survive being rooted up to 600 years. The tree, as a result, is very difficult to eradicate because at that depth it could continue to draw water from an underground source. Even cutting the tree to its base would not stop it from surviving. Offences in the heart can be so deeply rooted that it cannot be uprooted without strong faith that would prevent it from growing again. Unforgiveness and bitterness can have a devastating effect on an individual's spiritual life.

These detrimental attitudes that affect our spiritual life can be dealt with through forgiveness and faith in Jesus Christ. The scripture here is referring more to the kind of faith than the amount of faith required to deal with the problem of offence that is extremely resilient.

One of the most difficult things to do is for some people to forgive injuries that were done to them. Jesus, however, in speaking to Peter, made it abundantly clear that once forgiveness is requested, it must be given irrespective of how often you are offended. There should be no limit to the extending of forgiveness while guarding our hearts against retaliation, revenge, and toxic emotions.

Then Peter came to him and asked, "Lord, how often should I forgive someone who sins against me? Seven times?" "No, not seven times," Jesus replied, "but seventy times seven! (Matthew 18:21-22 - NLT).

Chapter 3

The Nature of Offence

"Individuals who deliberately decide not to take offence lead happier, more productive lives." —Lloyd D. Newell

An offended friend is harder to win back than a fortified city. Arguments separate friends like a gate locked with bars. (Proverbs 18:19 - NLT).

In many instances, offence cannot be avoided, and it can have a devastating effect on both the offended and the offender. The offended are usually described as hurt, wounded, upset, insulted, disappointed, irritated, angry, uncaring, frustrated, and vindictive. There is an extreme difficulty in reviving a friendship after offence has severed the bond. The offended party will resist all efforts at reconciliation. It is therefore necessary to ensure that one is blameless even if offence has been taken. Unresolved conflicts and contentions both separate and imprison the offended. It is therefore better to avoid rather than be subject to offences.

With reference to the process by which offence takes place, seven distinctive steps have been recognised:

1. Something happens.
2. The person perceives or feels that they have been wronged.
3. They take offence based on the incident.
4. The person becomes offended.
5. The offence remains unresolved.
6. The offence leads to resentment and subsequently anger.
7. The resentment and anger now lead to bitterness and the plot to revenge the wrong.

If these steps are not halted, then the victim can eventually become the victimiser. This is where an unhealed and hurting heart can endeavour to make others feel the same level of hurt and discomfort they have felt by inflicting hurt on others.

There are four ways in which the seed of offence is sown.

1. **What others have said to us.**

Words can have a particular damaging effect not only mentally but also emotionally. Many have been scarred by virtue of the hurt experienced by the things that have been said to them. The scarring may not be visible but emotional and psychological. This is especially true of children who may have a difficulty overcoming the effects of negative words spoken to them, especially by an authority figure.

A gentle answer deflects anger, but harsh words make tempers flare. (Proverbs 15:1 - NLT).

The above is generally true as expressed in the wisdom literature. Not responding to someone with the same emotional aggravation as they presented might help to temper the conversation and avoid extended conflicts. Sometimes it is not what is said but how it is said that creates the tension and ensuing resentment. However, as with so many things, there are exceptions to the rule. We can add fuel to an already explosive situation or provoke a person to wrath by being careless or vindictive with our words. Words have the potential for great harm or good, and much consideration must be given regarding choice of words and the tone used to express ourselves. There will however be occasions that no matter the attempts to appease by being gracious, the situation will still rapidly deteriorate. Great effort must be made to build up and not destroy others by our words. This can be done through speaking to edify, exhort and encourage.

2. **What others did not say to us.**

Many persons have been left distraught and devalued because both their actions and efforts have gone unappreciated. Much value is attached to simply saying thank you and not taking it for granted that your silence is an acknowledgment of gratitude. It is important to both affirm and acknowledge the contribution of others. This simple gesture can go a far way in giving individuals a sense of worth and value.

3. **What others did to us.**

The negative actions of others can lead to severe reactions from the offended. This is not limited to but involves feelings of betrayal and contributing to low self-esteem (worth). This is often the case, especially when done by persons we hold in high esteem.

It is not an enemy who taunts me—I could bear that. It is not my foes who so arrogantly insult me—I could have hidden from them. Instead, it is you—my equal, my companion and close friend. What good fellowship we once enjoyed as we walked together to the house of God. (Psalm 55:12-14 - NLT).

The above passage makes it clear that it is easier for those closest to us to cause offence. This happens because of the weight that we attach to interpersonal relationships. This makes us more vulnerable to offence and subsequently hurts. It is important that we stop storing up that which causes the cycle of pain and hurt.

4. **What others did not do for us.**

What can strike a cruel blow is unfulfilled expectations. Disappointments happen when promises are broken, or the wrong impression is given regarding same. We so often anticipate and expect others to treat us with the same level of love, concern, and appreciation that we would have given that we are left disappointed when it is not forthcoming.

Ways People Are Offended

1. **Innocently** – This happens when the offender is unaware of the impact of what they did or said has had on the offended.

2. **Thoughtlessly** – Not thinking about how others may be affected by our actions. Being careless with respect to the effects that our words or actions may have on others.

3. **Negative Response** – Using strong language to retaliate against those who caused us pain and anguish. Justifying our behaviour that they deserve what they got. Believing and stating the worst about others.

4. **Defensively** – Becoming so hurt that you do not allow others to get close to you. Viewing people with suspicion, which will affect your behaviour towards

them. Extremely protective of self to the exclusion of others.

5. **Deliberately** – Uncaring attitude. Not interested in the feelings of others, fully aware of the emotional pain and anguish your actions would have caused. Will intentionally hurt you to get ahead or to gain an advantage.

Six Types Of Offence

1. Taking Offence.
2. Giving Offence.
3. Offended by the truth.
4. Offended by God.
5. Offending the Holy Spirit (grieve).
6. Offending yourself (self-destructive).

The Effects Of Offence

Offence not only influences and affects the offender and offended, but even those who had nothing to do with the situation at hand. The mental and emotional state of the offended can affect how they treat with other interpersonal relationships. Below are some of the effects caused by offence:

- Have trouble in loving and worshipping because of the internal hurts and pains.
- Affects our prayer life and devotion to God.

- Results in us living in a state of unforgiveness.
- Time-consuming and affects our priorities.
- Can lead to deeper problems that is corrupting (bitterness, revenge, and hatred).
- Causes us to be both self-centered and selfish in our orientation. Offended because we cannot get our own way.
- Development of feelings of insecurity out of a sense of rejection.
- Constantly complaining and murmuring about people and situations.
- High maintenance relationship because we become difficult to please. Requires far more than the normal effort to maintain.
- Very contentious and argumentative. Display an unwillingness to settle disputes and grievances.
- Not open to instruction and guidance.
- Feeling that others are against you and so maintain distancing.
- The use of emotional blackmail as a means of revenge and retaliation.
- Deceptiveness revealed in appearing to be friendly but intending and making plans to hurt.
- Seeing what is not there and hearing what is not said.
- Highly misunderstood and mistreated.
- Allows pride to block from any source of help.
- Constantly depreciates the value and worth of others.
- Can be dangerous and attack others.

- Gathers and leads a group that is intent on hindering and/or destroying others.
- Will display levels of toxicity that make it difficult to be around them.

Chapter 4

Offence In Marriage

"In every disagreement in marriage, remember this one important truth: my spouse is my partner not my enemy. We will either win together or lose together." —Dave Willis

Lack Of Understanding

Offences are created in marriage primarily when there is a lack of understanding and ineffective communication—a lack of knowledge of our individual differences both physically and psychologically. When there is a lack of understanding of the individual's motivational needs, they remain unmet and breeds resentment and animosity. When there is also the lack of understanding of expectation in the relationship, couples strive to do what they assume is needed and offence is taken. All the above misunderstandings open the door for the onset of offences to be created in relationships.

Consider that men and women are intentionally created differently by the Creator. This is done so that we will both have a need for each other throughout the life of our marriage. There must be this sense of interdependence in your marriage so you will both have need of your strengths and vice versa to give longevity and harmony to your relationship. We must be aware of our individual motivational needs and how they are to be prioritized in our marriage, so we are never at cross-purposes in meeting our spouse's most felt needs.

We must also have an awareness of each other's expectations entering the union so we can eliminate creating or being an offence to our spouse when we fail to meet the expectation that we are unaware of. Ignorance in marriage, as in everything, is not bliss. God, through the prophet Hosea, warns *"My people suffer because of lack of knowledge" (see Hosea 4:6).* When there are unspoken expectations, failure to meet them will result in offence being taken. Misunderstandings give rise to offence, offence breeds resentment, and resentment gives way to anger, bitterness and other toxic behavioural tendencies. Lack of understanding can be altered by having conversations to seek for clarity. No one knows a person like themselves. Share with each other your preferences, your likes, and, similarly, your dislikes, and alleviate the monster of offence from your marriage. Knowledge is power!

Ineffective Communication

The second thing which leads to offence in marriage is ineffective communication. Just to note, couples are always communicating in marriage, even if they are not being verbal. The challenge then lies not in communicating itself but in ineffective communication in the marriage. There is a tendency with spouses to assume they know what their spouse's meant by what they emitted, but how the information is transmitted and received differs for each couple. Study has shown that assumptions are over 90% incorrect; so, to assume you know what your spouse meant without first seeking for clarity is exercising ignorance to the extent to which an offence may be caused or taken.

When couples are communicating, it is best to employ techniques that aid in sharing and listening effectively.

Conflict And Communication

Effective communication is the key to a good marriage or relationship. However, there are differences in the way partners relate to each other, which sometimes create tensions. Your understanding of how to manoeuvre through important decisions, trying times, and some amount of conflict will make the exchange of communication a lot easier. Completing the following questions can help to clarify some common communication issues.

Communication Techniques

WHEN SHARING

Focus On	Rather Than
One issue	Many issues
The problem	The person

Behaviour	Character
Specifics	Generalization
Expressions of feelings	Judgment of character
'I' statements	"You" statements
Observation of facts	Judgment of motives
Mutual understanding	Who's winning or losing

WHEN LISTENING

Focus On	**Rather Than**
The message content	The method of delivery
The meaning	The words
Clarification of valid points	Defense of incorrect accusation
Questions	Indications
Understanding	Judgment

There is non-verbal and verbal communication. What one takes away from the conversation is what causes the offence. Take a wife's need for feeling loved in a marriage. If she requires her husband to verbally tell her he loves her at a particular time and he ignores her request or makes a remark like "I don't have to tell you I love you or we wouldn't be married." This response can be taken by the wife to mean that he is avoiding the direct response because he really doesn't love her but does not want to tell her. By virtue of what is received by the wife, her greatest need of being loved is not felt.

Meanwhile, men communicate love by doing so the husband was not intending to hurt her by not verbally confessing his love. He may just be preoccupied with showing her in other provisional ways that he loves her and cannot understand why she needs to be told when it is clearly shown. The wife then takes offence to not 'being loved,' and the husband feels offended for his attempt at love being disregarded. We must be clear and specific in our communications to be effective. We must be careful not to leave room for assumptions. Even though we cannot always avoid the challenge of conflicts in our relationships, it is our responsibility to ensure we give attention to the protection of our marriage, so no offence is given knowingly and, hence, none taken.

Disagreements and challenges are never adequate reasons to opt out of a marriage and withdraw the canopy of love and respect for each other's feelings. Everyone enters a marriage to be first, and when our feelings are placed secondary to things and people, we take offence.

The first law of marriage is priority and with priority comes sacrifice and time. Make the sacrifice to relate in a way that communicates genuine care. Make the time to reassure each other that they are the most important person in the world, second to none. Never allow a wife to feel disrespected or unloved by virtue of what was deemed as an uncaring attitude. Never allow your spouse to feel the rigors of being tested to measure up. Rather than allow for assumptions, seek for clarity by reframing the conversations. Have sharing rather than accusative conversations, allowing your spouse to know how you are impacted by a word or action.

During this exercise of sharing, spouses listen attentively to each other without justifying behaviour only after which the apologies are given—apologizing because the intention was never to cause offence (hurt).

Intimacy And Offence

When offences are taken in marriage, it often leads to withdrawal of and from intimacy, which then causes a reciprocation, and intimacy built and shared is now eroded. Intimacy is best described as *into-me-see*. This means taking the time to know and be known, and sharing the depth of truth about each other that can never be otherwise known. The closeness shared in an intimate relationship builds a connection that is deep yet fragile because of the shared experiences and build-up of trust that the couple shares. Intimacy is also understood to mean different things based on socialization and, once again, because of the biological differences.

Men are from Mars and women are from Venus puts it quite succinctly. Intimacy for a woman is based on how she is treated by her spouse at any given time, and its flow can be easily disrupted if she does not feel loved. Because we primarily operate by our emotions, which is a fluctuating feeling, anything done or not done in accordance with our feelings creates a dissonance in our emotions which informs us that we have either done something wrong or we are no longer special or loved. When this happens, we take immediate offence based on our assumptions, and our spouse is greeted with this set of feelings often confused as to why we "have an attitude." We have disconnected because we feel hurt.

Disconnect of any sort can be an intimacy killer. For the female because of differences in how love and intimacy is perceived, and for the male because they are compartmentalized in their own emotions. These are both biological and psychological differences. These differences again are intentional for the synergizing of the marriage. It is meant to compliment and not complicate the relationship. For instance, men are created as providers of the home and family. If a conflict arises, a husband is still expected to maintain his provisional role and not be so affected by the conflict that it renders him incapable of providing. The female, because of the connectedness of her emotions, may still harbour mixed emotions based on the conflict and an offence is created that is not easily forgotten. This festers into resentment, and intimacy being eroded affects the harmony of the relationship. Engaging in a conversation will become necessary here to resolve the ill-feelings and set the differences aside so that we can control our individual emotions and get to the root cause of the offence.

Mastering Our Emotions

As individuals in a union, we must learn to master or control our emotions for the health of our marriage. Self-control is a fruit of the Spirit that is necessary in marriages. We cannot do as we always feel because we must consider that the marriage sustenance is the responsibility of both parties.

We must choose happy or honest at the expense of our deepest emotions. We will not always be able to avoid conflict but must choose how we react to them to minimize the effects on the marriage. Conflict itself does not hurt a relationship; it is the reactions that create the hurt which creates the offence.

We must be careful to think about the impact of our words and actions on our partners and our marriage. We have need to be wise as serpents and harmless (blameless) as doves (see Matthew 10:16) in our marriage. Being slow to speak and quick to listen (see James 1:19) highlights how the Lord frames what our actions ought to be. The law of physics denotes that for every action, there are equal and opposite reactions. There will be repercussions if offences are left unattended.

We must attempt delicate conversations with sensitivity. Culture and socialisation play an important role in our communication. We are products of our past, but we don't have to be prisoners to it. Let us, as couples representing Christ and His church, choose to make the necessary adjustments in our conversations, attitudes, and actions to avoid becoming an offence to each other and to Christ. It is important to make compromises where necessary because family dynamics and socialisation may vary. Let us be responsible for each other's emotional well-being and so fulfil the mission of Christ for our lives. Embody and exemplify the love and respect of Ephesians 5, emitting sacrificial and respectful love towards each other, submitting to each other in love with the understanding that submission is what you do willingly rather than what you are forced to do.

And further, submit to one another out of reverence for Christ. For wives, this means submit to your husbands as to the Lord. For a husband is the head of his wife as Christ is the head of the church. He is the Savior of his body, the church. As the church submits to Christ, so you wives should submit to your husbands in everything. For husbands, this means love your wives, just as Christ loved the church. He gave up his life for her to make her holy and clean, washed by the cleansing of God's word. He did this to present her to himself as a glorious church without a spot or wrinkle or any other blemish. Instead, she will be holy and without fault. In the same way, husbands ought to love their wives as they love their own bodies. For a man who loves his wife actually shows love for himself. No one hates his own body but feeds and cares for it, just as Christ cares for the church. (Ephesians 5:21-29 – NLT).

Submit to Lordship and leadership knowing that submission requires intelligent participation.

Wives, men are won by conduct if not conversation, therefore submitting is done not because you are wrong but because of his role. Godly conduct may win him over;

however, he may not concede to being wrong but demonstrate a change in behaviour. Don't always try to win the battle with words.

In the same way, you wives must accept the authority of your husbands. Then, even if some refuse to obey the Good News, your godly lives will speak to them without any words. They will be won over. (1 Peter 3:1 - NLT).

Husbands, 1 Peter 3:7 encourages that you dwell with her according to your understanding of her being the weaker vessel. Treat her with gentle care. It takes much strength to submit, especially in these unprecedented times of role-reversal.

Scriptures and other testimonial experiences reveal the level of influence the wife has in influencing the decision-making outcome of her husband. In the case of Adam and Eve, she was able to influence his decision to eat from the tree expressly forbidden by God.

The woman was convinced. She saw that the tree was beautiful and its fruit looked delicious, and she wanted the wisdom it would give her. So she took some of the fruit and ate it. Then she gave some to her husband, who was with her, and he ate it, too. (Genesis 3:6 – NLT).

This influence is further reflected in the relationship between Ahab and Jezebel. She was both manipulative and deceitful. She witnessed Ahab's disappointment in being turned down by Naboth concerning the procurement of his vineyard. Her response was to chide him, then take charge of the situation and, through craftiness, cause Naboth to be killed so her husband could gain possession.

His wife Jezebel came in and asked him, "Why are you so sullen? Why won't you eat?" He answered her, "Because I said to Naboth the Jezreelite, 'Sell me your vineyard; or if you prefer, I will give you another vineyard in its place.' But he said, 'I will not give you my vineyard.'" Jezebel his wife said, "Is this how you act as king over Israel? Get up and eat! Cheer up. I'll get you the vineyard of Naboth the Jezreelite." (1 Kings 21:5-7).

How we speak and our attitude can either continue or discontinue the cycle of offence. Apologising in humility will build bridges rather than erect walls. Understanding of each other's needs, expectation, and personality helps us to navigate better the potential minefields through conversation. It takes strength for a woman to submit. Biblical wisdom must be applied for her to submit. The woman should never submit to her husband, then resent and be disrespectful to him. One of the cornerstones of avoiding offence is mutual respect. Intelligent participation is required to fulfil the role of submission. This would speak to both an understanding and undertaking of the biblical role and responsibility.

Work It Out: How We Communicate

How do we talk to each other about difficult topics? What kind of guidelines can we establish to improve the quality of our communication?

Due to poor communication skills, couples often live with a fundamental misunderstanding of each other's feelings and pain, which causes you to fight and grow apart.

Case: *Nigel and Jackie were planning to get married. They were on a budget, so she ordered a simple but nice dress. Jackie was excited as she had waited for eight years and two children for Nigel to finally decide to marry. She had been working hard to lose some baby fat since the date was set six months earlier. She was already down eight pounds and wanted to lose another twelve pounds before the wedding, which was two months away. Nigel, who never had a weight issue, was always trying to be very supportive of her and didn't eat his nightly snacks in front of her.*

The dress she ordered arrived, and she tried on the dress in excitement and called Nigel into the room asking "So, what do you think?" Nigel froze in the doorway, unsure how to respond.

"What's wrong?" asked Jackie.

"Who said anything was wrong?" responded Nigel, "You look beautiful."

"I know you and I know when you are lying. Why did you hesitate? Doesn't it look good on me?" asked Jackie.

Nigel felt trapped. "You look great," he continued.

"Never mind," said Jackie unzipping the dress. "Forget I asked."

"What did I do?" asked Nigel.

"I just wanted the truth," responded Jackie.

"Well, the truth is that you look beautiful, but it looked a bit tight and may not look exactly the way you would want it to."

Jackie didn't respond, took off the dress and walked out of the room.

Oftentimes being in a marriage/relationship means standing at a pivotal intersection forced to choose between being happy and being honest about a response, and it creates tension and conflict. Every couple experiences this dynamic at some point or another, but conflict does not hurt our relationships. It just depends on how you argue and communicate, and whether understanding and kindness are at the core of the conversation.

Communication-wise, as couples, we fall into one of three major categories: **assertive/direct, conflict/avoidance,**

aggressive/passive-aggressive. Information in this section on communication styles has been heavily influenced by information obtained from the UK Violence Intervention and Prevention Center.

ASSERTIVE/DIRECT COMMUNICATION is a style in which individuals clearly state their opinions and feelings, and firmly advocate for their rights and needs without violating the rights of others. These individuals value themselves, their time, and their emotional, spiritual, and physical needs, and are strong advocates for themselves while being very respectful of the rights of others. They say what they think and feel, and the communication is marked by active listening and feedback. This method is straightforward and involves the two-way free-flowing sharing of thoughts, feelings, and ideas.

Assertive/Direct communicators will:

- State needs and wants clearly, appropriately, and respectfully.
- Express feelings clearly, appropriately, and respectfully.
- Use "I" statements.
- Communicate respect for others.
- Listen well without interrupting.
- Feel in control of self.
- Have good eye contact.
- Speak in a calm and clear tone of voice.

- Have a relaxed body posture.
- Feel competent and in control.
- Not allow others to abuse or manipulate them.
- Stand up for their rights.

This method of communication allows for the addressing of issues and problems as they arise, and creates a respectful environment for this interchange. They will recognise that we are equally entitled to respectfully express ourselves to each other. Assertiveness allows us to take care of ourselves and is fundamental for good mental health and healthy relationships.

Conflict avoidance is a person's method of reacting to conflict, which attempts to avoid directly confronting the issue at hand. This can include changing the subject, putting off a discussion until later or simply not bringing up the subject of contention.

CONFLICT AVOIDANCE/PASSIVE is a style in which individuals have developed a pattern of avoiding expressing their opinions or feelings, protecting their rights, and identifying and meeting their needs. As a result, passive individuals do not respond overtly to hurtful or anger-inducing situations. Instead, they allow grievances and annoyances to mount, usually unaware of the build-up. But once they have reached their high tolerance threshold for unacceptable behaviour, they are prone to explosive outbursts, which are usually out of proportion to the triggering incident. After the outburst, however, they may feel shame, guilt, and confusion, so they return to being passive.

Passive communicators will often:

- Fail to assert for themselves.
- Allow others to infringe on their rights deliberately or inadvertently.
- Fail to express their feelings, needs or opinions.
- Tend to speak softly or apologetically.
- Exhibit poor eye contact and slumped body posture.
- Often feel anxious because life seems out of their control.
- Often feel depressed because they feel stuck and hopeless.

AGGRESSIVE COMMUNICATION is a style in which individuals express their feelings and opinions and advocate for their needs in a way that violates the rights of others. Thus, aggressive communicators are verbally and/or physically abusive.

Aggressive communicators will often:

- Try to dominate others.
- Use humiliation to control others.
- Criticise, blame, or attack others.
- Be very impulsive.
- Have low frustration tolerance.

- Speak in loud, demanding, and overbearing voice.
- Act threateningly and rudely.
- Not listen well.
- Interrupt frequently.
- Use "you" statements.

They tend to blame others instead of owning their issues and tend to have an overbearing and intimidating posture. They often generate fear and hatred in others. They can be loud and pushy, commonly exhibiting a superior attitude. They tend to dominate, seeking to have their own way irrespective of.

PASSIVE AGGRESSIVE COMMUNICATION is a style where individuals appear to be passive on the surface but are really acting out anger in a subtle, indirect or behind-the-scenes way. The individual may appear to agree with the request but show anger and resentment through non-compliance.

Passive-Aggressive communicators will often:

- Mutter to themselves rather than confront the person or issue.
- Have difficulty acknowledging their anger.
- Use facial expressions that don't match how they feel (i.e., smiling when angry).
- Use of sarcasm.
- Deny there is a problem.

- Appear cooperative while purposely doing things to annoy and disrupt.
- Use subtle sabotage to get even.

It is easy for the passive-aggressive to be stuck in a situation of powerlessness and risk alienation from others. In many instances, they harbour resentment while the real issues at hand remain unresolved.

When you discuss your natural communication styles and establish rules for when to be direct and when to be avoidant, it will be much easier to navigate delicate conversations with sensitivity. Take the time to determine to which category you belong.

In the table below, Partner A (husband) will read each statement aloud, and Partner B (wife) will respond by answering whether the statement is "true" or "false" or "It's complicated" when it applies to her. After writing down all the answers, switch roles. Please exercise patience and try not to discuss your answers until you both have shared your responses.

Go Ahead! Try It!

1. I have thick skin; things don't easily bother me.
2. I grew up in a home where we shared our feelings openly.
3. I would always want you to tell me the truth, even if it hurts.

4. There are things you do and say sometimes that annoy me.
5. I am sensitive and easily offended.
6. Negative feedback really hurts me.
7. I have a deep need for approval.
8. I am comfortable telling people what I think, even if they don't like it.
9. I would rather bury my feelings than talk about them.
10. I am a people pleaser.

The answers you both wrote down will help to paint a picture of the sensitivities and differences of your communication styles. Take a few minutes now and ask the following questions of each other.

Are there any answers of mine that surprised you?

____

____

Where do our answers differ?

____

____

For those that you answered, "It's complicated," can you please explain what you mean?

____

____

____

What are some topics or situations that are generally sensitive for you?

____

____

____

How can I best approach a topic that might be sensitive for you?

____

____

____

If we were in Nigel and Jackie's situation, how might we best handle the situation?

____

____

____

What would feel comforting for you after we have an intense conversation?

____

____

____

Hold hands, pray together, husband leading the prayer: Ask God to give you understanding hearts and inner ears to listen with keen sensitivity, to know what is in the heart of your spouse, and wisdom to respond in difficult situations.

Now how about a hug.

Bishop Dr. Carla A. Dunbar B.Th., CST, LMFT, L.H.D., F.O.I.E., JP, OMS

Author, Personal Development Coach, Marriage, Family and Sex Counselling Therapist, CEO and Co-Founder of Carla Dunbar Ministries International

Chapter 5

Forgiveness: The Power To Heal From Offences

"An unhealed person can find offence in pretty much anything someone does. A healed person understands that the actions of others have absolutely nothing to do with them. Each day you get to decide which one you will be."
—Unknown

Many years ago, despite making a commitment to serve God and being actively engaged in singing in the choir, preaching several messages, and teaching the church school, I struggled with bitterness, pain and hurt yielded from past experiences. I resented the very thought of pardoning my offenders!

The posture of my heart then was relatable to that of what many people experience now. We find ways to feel good about and to justify our unforgiving heart rather than engage in the single most curative procedure called forgiveness. Engaging in a myriad of activities and performing well-needed roles does not excuse us from sharing in this life-changing and soul-searching process of forgiveness. There is no alternative to forgiveness. We must willingly and freely rid ourselves of the burden of yesterday while charting a path forward, characterized by love, peace, harmony, and goodwill.

A sincere donation of pardon has the propensity to restore happiness and wholesomeness to the donor. It removes the catastrophic pain and deep-seated grudge from the heart. Treat yourself today to a happier you.

Let all bitterness and wrath and anger and clamor [perpetual animosity, resentment, strife, fault-finding] and slander be put away from you, along with every kind of malice [all spitefulness, verbal abuse, malevolence]. Be kind and helpful to one another, tender-hearted [compassionate, understanding], forgiving one another [readily and freely], just as God in Christ also forgave you. (Ephesians 4:31-32 - AMP).

Unforgiveness traps us in the pain of the past, disrupting each day with thoughts of dissatisfaction, and minimizing any hope of a fulfilled tomorrow. Seize the moment to assess and heal the wounds that greatly influence and affect you. Make a deliberate attempt to release yourself from the bondages of the past and glorify God through your will to restore and build healthy relationships.

The donor's right to forgiveness is directly correlated to his or her will to freely absolve even the undeserving.

For if you forgive other people when they sin against you, your heavenly Father will also forgive you. But if you do not forgive others their sins, your Father will not forgive your sins. (Matthew 6:14-15 - NIV).

Findings from a recent study suggest that people sometimes withhold forgiveness because of the perception that the offender is guilty and undeserving. Forgiveness is unconditional. Our offenders do not need to qualify for our forgiveness, neither do they need to earn it. Instead, we should willingly supply where there is a need. We must be eager to share forgiveness with others characterized by the love of Christ displayed on the cross if we are to enjoy the luxury of forgiveness. Though not easy, it is right to forgive. One can only consider him or herself pure if he is willing to release those responsible for our agony.

I recall that during my formative years, I was intent on suppressing forgiveness from my offenders. It is said that "The faintest ink is better than the strongest memory." Being cognisant of this, I solidified the memory by making a written account of the offences, offenders, and the verdicts to be imposed for each transgression. Can you relate to this type of thinking?

I thought that keeping the precious gift of forgiveness from my offenders would give me a sense of self-gratification and renewed power. Instead, the pain prevailed even greater. It was consistent and grew even more overwhelming. Even the faintest joy would dwindle at the sight or thought of an offender. I felt bound and distressed. The constant suffering no doubt affected me more than my offenders. Daily, the unease magnified while my trespasser went about unbothered.

I can concur with Marianne Williamson that *"Unforgiveness is like drinking poison and waiting for the other person to die."* It is imperative that we break the vicious cycle of unforgiveness and discontinue the bondage of malice.

"To forgive is to set a prisoner free and discover that the prisoner was you." —Lewis B. Smedes

Now is the time to purposely engage in therapy. The surgeon of the soul is on duty, ready to heal the dysfunctionalities caused by yesterday's pain. You must willingly partake in the procedure. Let go of the past hurt and release your offender today.

The intricacies of each recording I made would bring back to memory the tales of the suffering and abuse of a teenage boy. Like a stalwart English scholar, the pen detailed the who, what, when, where, why and how. Each day I relived the horror of what was said and done to me. I was trapped behind "these prison walls." The only difference was that I had the keys to freedom, peace, joy, and true happiness, though I was reluctant to use it.

Forgiveness is not always easy. At times, it feels more painful than the wound we suffered, to forgive the one that inflicted it. Yet, there is no peace without forgiveness.

"Forgive others, not because they deserve forgiveness, but because you deserve peace." —Marianne Williamson

Forgiveness is instant, but the healing of the wound is progressive and requires ongoing submission to God and His Word. Forgiveness, though miraculously heal those who are broken, is not the result of mystery but decision. We must decide to free our offenders, those we have been safely grilled (imprisoned) in our maximum-security facilities (hearts); those who have no hope for parole. Prisoners require guards to host them. Relinquish your post as guard commander by dismissing the charges against those who have violated you. Forgiveness sets both the prisoner and the guard free. Let us take hold of our freedom today.

"For to be free is not merely to cast off one's chains, **but to live in a way that respects and enhances the freedom of others."** —Nelson Mandela

The time is now for us to do a heart evaluation. What is the status of your heart? We must withhold gifts, pause the spiritual performances, and do an introspection of the heart.

"So if you are presenting a sacrifice at the altar in the Temple and you suddenly remember that someone has something against you, leave your sacrifice there at the

altar. Go and be reconciled to that person. Then come and offer your sacrifice to God." (Matthew 5:23-24 – NLT).

It is far more fulfilling to forgive an offender than it is to participate in religious duty. Our services to God do not justify our poor treatment of others. Jesus affirms the importance of forgiveness during this exposition of the Lord's prayer: *"and forgive us our sins, as we have forgiven those who sin against us." (Matthew 6:12 - NLT).*

"Once our eyes have been opened to see the enormity of our offence against God, the injuries which others have done to us appear by comparison extremely trifling. If, on the other hand, we have an exaggerated view of the offences of others, it proves that we have minimized our own." (Stott, cited in Carson).

Unforgiveness imprisons the offended with ongoing anger, hurt, and bitterness, thus deters any hope of sincere growth and spiritual development. Unforgiveness is choosing to stay trapped in a jail cell of bitterness, serving time for someone else's crime.

"When boiled down to its essence, unforgiveness is hatred."
—John R. Rice

Forgiveness is not limited to a private confession with God. It is the purposeful decision to set the offender free and to close the case against him or her without the possibility for a recall of this matter in the future. It is being willing to let go; that is, no intention to demand payment for the outstanding debt. Forgiveness is definitely and decisively the path to true freedom. No one can truly claim to be free while refusing to drop charges mounted against others. Peace and satisfaction are the result of true forgiveness.

Forgiveness requires bold and relentless trust in God and His promises. Unaware of this, I continued to participate in activities that proved my uprightness. Detouring to avoid collision will only result in a longer route to the starting point of forgiveness. There is no shortcut to inner freedom; liberty is only attained when one is bold enough to believe in God and drop the charges. Unforgiveness is the clearest illustration that depicts the unsurrendered heart that is too doubtful to trust God and His prescription to heal. We are taught by scripture to be tolerant of one another and forgive each other. If anyone has a complaint against another, just as the Lord has forgiven you, you also should forgive (see Colossians 3:13).

Ignoring the symptoms of unforgiveness does not prove deliverance and completeness; rather, it affirms that one is imprisoned by his or her own selfishness to share with another something one has received freely and are also continuously in need of. Mark 11:25 postulates that *"But when you are praying, first forgive anyone you are holding a grudge against, so that your Father in heaven will forgive your sins too." (NLT)*. Unforgiveness is inexcusable and is detrimental to wholesome Christianity.

I shouted several praises across varying services and prayed in a manner that impressed many, but deep down I suffered from unforgiveness. I knew this because I found solace and a sense of satisfaction in the evident pain of my offenders. I felt satisfied knowing that there was something so precious as "my forgiveness" that they needed that I had the power to deny. Forgiveness is the best medicine you can give to yourself; the opposite is to slowly destroy peace and sanity.

Forgiveness requires action. May you grow weary of living in bitterness and anger today. Forgiveness is urgent and should never be withheld for some other convenient time. Not only does it lead to feelings of stress, anxiety, depression, insecurity, and fear, but it impedes your relationship with others and God.

One evening, as I reflected on the great forgiveness extended to us as shared in the scripture: *"as far as the east is from the west, so far has he removed our transgressions from us" (Psalms 103:12 - NIV),* I decided permanently to release those who had hurt me. There and then I chose to replace the bitterness with love. With tears descending from my cheek, I knelt and prayed for God's grace. I soon remembered the book that bore the record of the accounts of the offences and the offenders. That evening I tore the pages out over an open fire as I said goodbye to my former pain and welcomed peace, freedom, and tranquillity. May you rid yourself of every reminder of yesterday's pain. Deliberately take hold of your freedom to live a fulfilled life.

Let us pray: *Father, help me to pardon those who have offended me. Reveal to me anything lingering that could hold me hostage to the pains of the past. Give me the grace to heal through this process, in Jesus' Name. Amen.*

I soon learned that releasing offenders was more beneficial to me. I was no longer uncomfortable in their presence.

"If you love me, obey my commandments." (John 14:15 - NLT).

Love is not a mere reaction to perceived goodness but rather a commitment to action. Your love for God should be highlighted with much grace and excitement every time there is an opportunity to pardon an individual. There is never a bad time to offer love. Similarly, every day is a season for engaging in active forgiveness. Forgiveness is the medication for dealing with hurt, rejection, anger, and bitterness. Take regular dosage for a happier you.

In Genesis 29:31, we meet Leah, the older of Laban's daughters. She was given to marry Jacob, a young man in pursuit of her younger sister, Rachel, because their father considered it important to honour the custom of the day, which was to ensure that the eldest daughter was the first to be married. Clearly, Jacob had no desire or love for Leah. From the onset, he was willing to work for Rachel and, even after he was given Leah, he was committed to do whatever it took to marry Rachel. Leah was stuck with a husband with whom she did not ask to marry and one who did not find her desirable. This possibly led to her feeling hurt, used, mishandled, and bitter. Leah was simply the victim of her offender's choice.

Sometimes the greatest hurt amounts from the involuntary suffering we face. Furthermore, forgiving becomes more challenging because you are perceived as the aggressor, troublemaker, and inconsiderate person. Though difficult, try to set your offender free. This will result in you being released from the bondage of the past hurt, disappointment, and bitterness of life. Resign yourself from the prison of your past circumstances, despite your feelings.

Forgiving your offender does not always mean we will feel better immediately, but as with prescribed medication, the signs of bitterness and unhealed trauma will begin to fade even from our subconscious memory. True forgiveness will erase the details of the hurt and pain it caused with time. Therefore, forgiveness is both instantaneous and progressive.

Your decision to pardon is a plan to heal permanently. Forgiveness withheld affects both you and others to include those you care most about. Additionally, it creates enmity between you and God. A day away from God is a day without peace, strength, joy, and happiness. Introspect today, as the absence of peace and harmony are the warning signs of unforgiveness.

Sometimes past hurt affects our present decisions holding us as hostages to the past. Simply ignoring or developing a positive mindset about yesterday's pain does not guarantee full freedom. Rather, it reinforces the need to forgive quickly. Take, for instance, Leah. With the hope of a brighter tomorrow, she got pregnant and gave her husband a son, Reuben. Though she anticipated that this would be the end of her humiliation and suffering, it proved to be a mere continuation.

Leah conceived and gave birth to a son and named him Reuben (See, a son!), for she said, "Because the LORD has seen my humiliation and suffering; now my husband will love me [since I have given him a son]." (Genesis 29:32 - AMP).

The effects of unforgiveness will only terminate when you make a deliberate step to pardon your offenders. The pain is unbearable; therefore, make an urgent appointment to have this matter resolved. Sometimes searching for love and acceptance from the persons who offend us will prove futile. Forgiveness does not mean the pursuit of your offender's love and appreciation; it simply means settling the outstanding debts. Forgiving your offender will not always result in a transformed relationship; it means progression to restoration, hope, and inner peace. How much longer will you remain hostage within the bars of pain and bitterness? Come out today and free yourselves from the emotional trauma. The longer you take to pardon, extends the duration of the trauma.

Leah later had a second son, hoping to grasp the attentive ear of her offender. Forgiving does not require the person to listen or even accept your gift of forgiveness; it is an involuntary gift that we hope will be graciously received.

Then she conceived again and gave birth to a son and said, "Because the LORD heard that I am unloved, He has given me this son also." So, she named him Simeon (God hears). (Genesis 29:33 - AMP).

Our traumatic experiences are contagious, and the effects often transcend to those we love such as our children. Get vaccinated today against the ills of unforgiveness. Unforgiveness creates room in our cages for others and invites them to become proud hostages of our pain and hurt. Can you imagine all the hurtful expressions Leah must have voiced to her children concerning the treatment of her husband? "Your dad does not love me." "He is only abusing me." "I am suffering!"

As a child, I grew up hating people to whom I had never once spoken to in my life. I had a poor relationship with my father after listening to all the horrors shared by my mother. Your children are innocent. Forgive today so they can experience a peaceful today and a joyful tomorrow. A decision to forgive is an investment in the peace of others, especially those you care about. Your pain is contagious, and it is affecting those you care most about.

Your next step should be to forgive. Prolonged unforgiveness leads to further hurt, pain, and bitterness. Perhaps Leah's excuse was that they were the ones who rejected her, so it was their responsibility to console her. Forgiveness is your responsibility. You are the steward over your life. God made you a manager. Make a decision that will enhance your peace and happiness.

Sometimes we hold on to the hurt believing that we are victims and we don't belong. Forgiveness joins us immediately to God's friendship plan. What are you waiting for? Leah's delay resulted in a third son, simply hoping for an experience of companionship.

She conceived again and gave birth to a son and said, "Now this time my husband will become attached to me [as a companion], for I have given him three sons." Therefore, he was named Levi. (Genesis 29:34 - AMP).

Your actions highlight where you suffer most. Record the signs and engage in the process of forgiveness today. The purpose of the diagnosis is to reveal the symptoms to be addressed. Ignoring the symptoms leads to more trauma.

Leah had a fourth son which highlights that unforgiveness not only affects you and others but also your relationship with God.

"Again, she conceived and gave birth to a [fourth] son, and she said, "Now I will praise the LORD." So she named

him Judah; then [for a time] she stopped bearing [children]. (Genesis 29:35 - AMP).

Clearly, she decided to worship God. True worship is an act of the heart characterized by extreme submission to God. Though not stated, we can infer that Leah finally decided to pardon her offenders and was now able to genuinely praise God. Worship is undone without sincere pardon.

But when you are praying, first forgive anyone you are holding a grudge against, so that your Father in heaven will forgive your sins, too. (Mark 11:25 - NLT).

Worship cannot be considered serious unless it is offered by people who have first been forgiven. If praise is about celebrating, then bitter, sad, depressed, revengeful and unforgiving people are incapable of genuinely undertaking this activity. Leah halted childbearing for a while and became engaged in the healing process of forgiveness. Her actions were characterized by praise and honour. True forgiveness brings deliverance.

May you take steps to bring a resolution to the disease of unforgiveness. You deserve to sleep comfortably, worship genuinely, and live purposefully. Forgive today so you can experience joy beyond the walls of your heart.

Finally, here is your prescription to a better you:

1. **Introspect:** Who caused the hurt? What is it that is affecting you?
2. **Pray:** ask God for wisdom.
3. **Connect with the source of your hurt:** Locate the person or persons. Engage them in a discussion, if you can.
4. **Let it go:** Let the person or persons know they are free.
5. **Gratitude:** Thank the person for listening and thank God for an opportunity to make things right.
6. **Full speed ahead:** Move forward believing God's Word that forgiveness is best.
7. **Ongoing Praise:** Use every day as a day of praise that you made it out of the trauma room of bitterness.
8. **Do it repeatedly:** This is for perfection and maturity.

Rev. Nicholas Robertson

Dip. Min (hon), Dip. Ed. (hon), BD (hon), B.Ed. (hon), Med. (hon)
Author, Co-Founder/Director of Impact Online Bible Institute, Founder Positive Vibration 365 Plus, Founder and COO of BuildAMan Foundation Ltd.,

Chapter 6

The Psychology Of Offence

"Life appears too short to be spent nursing animosity or registering wrongs." —Charlotte Bronte.

Offence, according to Poggi & Derrico, is referred to as a feeling that is "triggered by a blow to a person's honour" because it contradicts a person's self-concept and identity. Feeling offended belongs to the "self-conscious emotions" like shame, guilt, and pride, and like shame and humiliation, it is caused by a blow to the person's image and self-image.

Being offended can cause one to feel empowered in that it allows others to feel guilty, thereby putting the offended in a position of power. Taking offence can cause one to avoid both vulnerability and the real problem at the root of their pain.

Clashes Of Expectations Or Values

Whenever expectations are breached, the disappointment can lead to offence. These interpersonal expectations can influence relationships in various ways.

Foreseeability expectations – This causes us to expect others to predict the potentially negative impact that their words or actions may have simply because we think that they know us well (I did not expect to hear this from my friend).

Reciprocity expectations – This is based on the hope that favours, gifts, or other acts of kindness will be returned in kind (I stopped sending him birthday wishes because he keeps forgetting mine).

Equity expectations – These are about our desire to be treated fairly and equally (It offends me how mom always stands up for my sister but not me).

Offence can also be taken outside of our personal relationships. Offence can be taken at social media comments that ridicules or questions matters that are of value or importance to us. These can include but are not limited to religion, ethnic grouping, politics, and values. Our accumulated experiences through life can make us more prone to being affected or influenced by our understanding of what is being said, which affects our beliefs, values, and expectations. It is possible therefore to lash out in defence of the values that you uphold. This can perpetuate a cycle of causing and taking offence.

Offence can be rooted in ignorance concerning what affects you and why. Society, rather than expecting persons to learn to deal with minor conflicts and differences in opinion, tends to reward hypersensitivity. Social media support can be garnered by playing the victim or appearing to be offended by the actions of others. Users tend to feel vindicated simply by speaking out about the offences encountered reinforcing the belief that their experiences were particularly harmful and traumatic.

Taking offence at someone's actions or words is a choice you make. Offence can have a profound effect on your mental well-being and sense of self-worth. To make matters worse, it can cause others to be ultra-sensitive when around the offended party. When you put yourself in a position of being constantly offended, it can create a sense of paranoia with respect to how you are viewed by others. Remember not to always assume that what is being said is meant to be offensive to you. It is important to shake the label of being a perpetual victim where you avoid anything that makes you uncomfortable or fearful. It is not healthy to live life in a state of constant morbid fears.

Realigning Sensitivity

- Stop assuming the negative intent by giving people the benefit of the doubt. You lose objectivity when you train yourself to take offence often about minor issues.

- Offence does not equal harm. Nothing physical has happened to you. Stop allowing yourself to be hammered and feeling like a casualty always through your real-life experiences.

- You need to consider carefully why you are upset and take time and thought to provide a perspective on what was the basis for your actions.

- You may need to change your personal expectations of others. They may be oblivious to what is influencing or affecting you. They may not even feel that they have contributed to you feeling offended.

- Unless the speaker basically addresses you, don't assume that what was said was meant for you. Remember, everything you hear cannot always be about you. Do not allow your thoughts to be infiltrated by this level of reasoning.

- It is important to address or confront the issue at hand before deciding if what was said was a deliberate attempt to offend you. You either discuss it or let it go. Guard yourself against becoming hypersensitive to an issue by making a choice not to become overly sensitive.

- When you choose to be offended, you start majoring in self-hurt and cause others to be ultra-sensitive around you or simply avoid you. It is important that you pick your battles carefully because not everything is worth the fight.
- Do not allow what happens to you in life to control or manipulate how you feel and react.

How To Deal With The Offended

- Confirm your suspicions whether the person was offended or taken aback by asking the right questions concerning a possible change of attitude.

- Clear up all misconceptions concerning the intent of words or actions rather than leaving it unattended.

- Ask questions to ensure that what was said was what was heard and interpreted.

- Carefully and sincerely observe to determine what was the cause of their concern and how it affected them.

- Once they reveal their perspective, ensure that you make them aware that you understood.

- Let them see and understand your perspective that no harm was intended.

- You may need to adjust or frame what you do differently in the future to create better harmony relationally.

- You may not agree but be respectful to the person during the conversation.

- Be ready to learn so that the relevant change or adjustments can be made.

Chapter 7

Offences In The Early Church

"A fool contributes nothing worth hearing and take offence at everything." —Aristotle

Dealing With Issues Of Abandonment

Both the first century Church, and the Church in this century, are not devoid of offences. The differences in how humans behave will potentially always have an effect or put a strain on interpersonal relationships. Many offensive situations have been caused by personality clashes and differences of opinions.

After some time Paul said to Barnabas, "Let's go back and visit each city where we previously preached the word of the Lord, to see how the new believers are doing." Barnabas agreed and wanted to take along John Mark. But Paul disagreed strongly, since John Mark had deserted them in Pamphylia and had not continued with them in their work. Their disagreement was so sharp that they separated. Barnabas took John Mark with him and sailed for Cyprus. Paul chose Silas, and as he left, the believers entrusted him to the Lord's gracious care. Then he traveled throughout Syria and Cilicia, strengthening the churches there. (Acts 15:36-41 - NLT).

Being a Christian does not exempt you from having strong opinions concerning people or situations. Sometimes the matter might not be brought to an amicable solution, especially when emotions run high. The reality may not be one of forgiveness but rather a lack of trust that the matter that caused the problem may resurface. Where issues of trust remain, it is difficult to effect reconciliation. The difficulty may also stem from neither party being willing to concede but holding strongly to their point of view. Both parties may have a reason for their opinion that appears to be valid, however unable to reach a resolution.

In this case, the dispute between Paul and Barnabas concerned John Mark. It was reported that he had deserted the Apostle and left the work because of the apparent fruitlessness. His seeming lack of resolve made Apostle Paul adamant that he was unsuitable. Barnabas however was of the view that he could still be useful despite the earlier abandonment. The result was an explosive situation because of the strong disagreement regarding same. Paul was obviously offended by the lack of courage and endurance of John Mark and was unwilling to give him a second chance at what he perceived would be the same outcome. Let us be aware that in matters where there is a difference of opinion, we can disagree without becoming disagreeable. Difference of opinion does not have to be taken personally. Deal with the issues but leave the personality out of it.

The sharp disagreement led to them parting ways. John Mark went with Barnabas, and Silas went with Paul. Offence can lead to an unwillingness to forgive the failings of others and to give another opportunity for training and development. Offence can result, as in this case with Paul and John Mark, in a lack of trust. It would not be prudent to go on a mission with someone you do not trust. The problem could also stem from short-sightedness or not having the patience or temperament to deal with the type of failings observed. Barnabas saw potential, but Paul saw problems. However, in this case, the conflict resulted in more purposeful ministry by both parties.

The disappointment we feel towards the failings of others might not have a quick fix but, given time, the healing of the rift can take place. Paul's view was a noble one and extended to the importance of the work ethic required for ministry. Barnabas, on the other hand, recognised that given another opportunity, it was possible for John Mark to turn around and be able to offer an invaluable contribution. We must always leave ourselves open for forgiveness, restoration, and reconciliation, especially when we partner with the Holy Spirit. He can quell long-standing disputes and adversities. It is important that we never say never, and so prolong the hostility towards each other when God wants to work on the heart of both the offended and offender.

Sometimes the persons that offend us today can become an invaluable asset and help tomorrow. There is a folly sometimes in permanently disconnecting from those who have offended us because we are unable to see the reality of their contributions in the future or the prospects of their future development. There must be those among us who will stand by and help in the restoration of the offenders. The offenders may bleed and hurt as much as the offended. With time and strategic involvement geared at restoration and recovering, those once considered liabilities can become a tremendous asset towards the work of the Kingdom of God.

Only Luke is with me. Bring Mark with you when you come, for he will be helpful to me in my ministry. (2 Timothy 4:11 - NLT).

The above passage clearly illustrates that with time the value of John Mark came to the forefront, totally reversing the earlier effects that caused the initial offence. Paul was now happy to receive his ministry as he recognised the benefits that would accrue. Never allow offence to blind you to the potential of others. The value and contribution of some will be revealed later than others. It is important also that the offender learn to move beyond the treatment meted out which at the time might seem insensitive and distanced. We must give those who have caused offence an opportunity to demonstrate genuine repentance for their actions. Those seeking for forgiveness must be granted it irrespective of the nature and severity of the offence. The offender must be given an opportunity to mature in his walk with God under the careful guidance and supervision of a more mature believer.

We learn from this experience with Paul and John Mark that:

1. The past mistakes we have made in offending others do not define our future but speak to our past.

2. Making a mistake by offending others in life or ministry does not mean it is all over, but you can get back in the game.

3. Be opened to reconnect and re-establish a relationship with others that was previously lost through offence.

4. Even when you have been let down by others, it's never too late to forgive and to take the next move forward. If we can change, others can too.

5. The person who hurt you in the past may be an invaluable asset in your future.

6. Renewal and reconciliation are still possible even after a strong dissension.

7. Breaches that create offences can be healed.

Dealing With Discrimination

It is often very challenging to show parity in all our interpersonal relationships. The believing community has been shown to certainly not be exempt in this regard. Discrimination has to do with the unjust or prejudicial treatment of different categories of people. According to Merriam Webster, it is the practice of unfairly treating a person or group of people differently from other people or groups.

But as the believers rapidly multiplied, there were rumblings of discontent. The Greek-speaking believers complained about the Hebrew-speaking believers, saying that their widows were being discriminated against in the daily distribution of food. (Acts 6:1 - NLT).

It is a natural part of growth and expansion that friction increases. The more persons you have interacting on a personal level, the greater the potential for offence. The rumblings of discontent evidenced in this passage was primarily due to what was conceived as discrimination and partiality. The Greek-speaking widows felt that they were being unfairly treated and complained about the apparent disparity. Feelings of neglect and bias are always a fertile ground for the germination and proliferation of offence.

With unfair treatment, one can either internalise or speak out against it. Fear of reprisal can cause one to be discontented but unwilling to vocalise. It is important that dialogue be initiated to deal with the threat to Christian harmony of partiality rather than to suffer in silence and risk becoming bitter within the heart. Offence always tends to imprison the offended party. There is much to be gained by speaking up and working towards an amicable solution.

Dealing With Discrepancies

We will never be free from dealing with issues that give rise to the creation of offences. It is evident that the early church had to find new and innovative ways to deal with these discrepancies.

But when Peter came to Antioch, I had to oppose him to his face, for what he did was very wrong. When he first arrived, he ate with the Gentile believers, who were not circumcised. But afterward, when some friends of James came, Peter wouldn't eat with the Gentiles anymore. He was afraid of criticism from these people who insisted on the necessity of circumcision. As a result, other Jewish believers followed Peter's hypocrisy, and even Barnabas was led astray by their hypocrisy. (Galatians 2:11-13 – NLT).

Prejudice and biases have been a major factor in causing offences. These by their very nature are discriminatory as it esteems one group above the other and then singles them out for special treatment.

Relationships can be marred by inconsistencies in how we deal with each other. Our moral compass that determines what is wrong or right cannot purely be situational.

The unmasking of the hypocrisy demonstrated by Peter was crucial if the church was going to deal with this obvious bias to real brotherhood. People get hurt and may become resentful, especially when persons in authority have not been transparent.

Dealing With Those Seeking To Discredit

Paul had to deal with the issue of being targeted in a very unusual way. To discredit and undermine him, some were using ministry to add to the burden of his imprisonment. There was also the blatant attack on his apostleship and teachings.

It's true that some are preaching out of jealousy and rivalry. But others preach about Christ with pure motives. They preach because they love me, for they know I have been appointed to defend the Good News. Those others do not have pure motives as they preach about Christ. They preach with selfish ambition, not sincerely, intending to make my chains more painful to me. (Philippians 1:15-17 - NLT).

God in His graciousness and sovereignty was using this experience of Paul's imprisonment and the impure motives of his rivals for the advancement of the gospel. Paul was neither discouraged by his current situation nor offended by those who were using his messages in a deliberate attempt to inflame his enemies. He was unperturbed by those competing to become more popular preachers considering his adversarial condition.

Paul however recognised that even if their motive was dishonourable, the result of the gospel message reaching its intended audience was being achieved. So, his lack of physical liberty was made more bearable in the fact that the Word of God was not bound but freely delivered. Paul refused to be offended by the personal attack and charges laid against him that was intended to affect both his ministry and sphere of influence.

Chapter 8

Overcoming Childhood Offence: Dealing With the Mother/Father Wounds

"Our response to an offence determines our future." —John Bevere

As Katie sat with her 80-year-old mother for their usual weekly Sunday visit and dinner, she said, "Mom, I have my second session with my therapist this week."

"Oh, he's going to tell you all the reasons why you should hate me," her mom answered curtly.

She replied, "No, mom. He's already aware of that. He's trying to fix it."

Even with the best of intentions, parents of different races, classes and cultures have for, as long as humans have existed, inflicted deep emotional wounds, and left scars they often knew nothing about. In this chapter, we will explore the issue of offence in the context of the parent-child relationship, commonly referred to by psychologists as the "mother wound" and "father wound."

The Mother Wound

According to British psycho-analyst Donald Winnicott, there is no such thing as an infant, but only an infant and their mother. He believed that a child's sense of self is built by the kind of relationship they have with their primary caregiver (usually mom). The best way to think of the mother wound is a loss or a lack of mothering; a deficit in the connection and nurturing that should flow from a mother to a child.

Any significant persistently negative interaction or lack of a meaningful connection between a mother and child can result in emotional and psychological wounds that can affect the child throughout their life span.

Causes Of The Mother Wound

The following are factors that can lead to a child having a mother wound:

- Alcoholic or drug-addicted mother.
- Mentally ill mother (undiagnosed or untreated).
- Emotionally distant mother.
- Mother carrying her own unhealed mother wound.
- Absent mother.

- Death of a mother early in life.
- Abusive mother; physical, verbal, or emotional.
- Being given up by mother to be raised by someone else.
- Migration of mother.
- Neglect.
- A hurting mother who complains to her child, making the child her confidante and counsellor.

The mother wound is often a silent infection of the soul (mind, will and emotions) that becomes very pervasive, affecting how that individual relates to others, interprets his/her experiences, and responds to stimuli in his/her environment.

Signs Of A Mother Wound

If you are carrying a mother wound, you may be able to look back on your childhood and identify issues such as:

- Never feeling that you had your mother's approval or acceptance; feeling like you missed the mark or you were never good enough.
- Being concerned about not being loved by your mother or that she loved your siblings more.
- Difficulties being emotionally open and honest with your mother.
- Always trying to gain her acceptance and attention by trying to do better or to be perfect.

- Feeling like a burden, a problem, or a bother to your mother.
- Feeling the need to protect, care for or shelter your mother rather than her doing those things for you.

Effects Of The Mother Wound

Let me make it abundantly clear that both sons and daughters can be affected significantly by a mother wound because we were all made with the need to be nurtured and accepted by our mothers. Any deficit in that need being met is a threat to our emotional and spiritual well-being. Some of the possible effects are:

- Low self-esteem and/or self-hate.
- Inability to maintain healthy relationships.
- Difficulty expressing and receiving love.
- Being easily offended.
- Trust issues; difficulty trusting others.
- Feeling incomplete.
- Lack of empathy.
- Perfectionism.
- Unrealistic high standards for self and others.
- Co-dependency.
- Feeling competitive with other women.
- People pleasing; a cry for acceptance and approval.
- Self-sabotage: having self-defeating habits and thoughts that hinder one from reaching their goals.
- High tolerance for poor treatment from others.

- Mental health issues such as eating disorders, depression, anxiety, and addictions.

The Father Wound

The father wound is a somewhat familiar concept to many persons in the Western world due to a long-standing social problem of father absenteeism. In addition, many children have had to live with the pain of being rejected by a father who may have said openly "That's not my child."

The physical or emotional absence of a father from a child's life is one of the main causes of the father wound. A father who is present but overly critical, negative or abusive towards his child can also inflict the father wound. Like the mother wound, it has the power to affect all areas of an individual's life, particularly his or her self-esteem, resilience, relational skills, and general outlook on life. Simply put, the father wound is the intentional or unintentional absence of love from your birth father.

Causes Of The Father Wound

The father wound can be the result of:

- Abuse: physical, emotional, mental, sexual, or verbal.
- Absence: this may be because of abandonment, divorce, separation, death, or busyness.

- Addiction: this can cause a rift in the father-child relationship and have long-term negative effects.
- Neglect: father's failure to own the child or provide the necessary care, acceptance, and affirmation that we all need from our fathers.
- Inability of the father to express and receive love because of his own unhealed emotional wounds.

Signs And Symptoms Of The Father Wound

You may have experienced the father wound if you can identify with any of the following experiences:

- Your father didn't spend time with you.
- Your father disapproved of your beliefs and/or your behaviours.
- You were afraid of your father.
- Your father was physically or emotionally absent.
- Food, love, and other necessities were withheld from you as punishment by your father.
- You find it difficult to trust males.
- Your father was highly critical of you.
- You avoid going to or never go to your father with personal problems.
- You feel abandoned or disowned by your father.
- You feel you need to be perfect to please him.

The Possible Effects Of The Father Wound

- Negative attitudes and beliefs about males.

- Flawed view of God as Father.
- Promiscuity; sometimes in search of a father's love.
- Unhealthy relationships with older men or men in authority.
- Aggressive behaviour.
- Deep rooted anger and resentment.

The role of a parent is extremely critical. You and I are in some way or another the product of our interactions with our parents or the lack of it. Our children will be the products of our interactions with them. For the cycle of offence to be broken, it must be understood and confronted.

Being Healed From The Mother/Father Wound

Here are ten steps you can take as you pursue freedom from the mother/father wound:

1. ***Admit that you are wounded.*** The first step in getting help is to admit that you need help. Allow yourself to come to grips with the fact that you did not receive all you needed from your parent(s) as a child. Process that by allowing yourself to feel and express the emotions that come with accepting the reality of what you have been through. You may use a journal to write your thoughts, or you can record yourself talking about it. This activity is not so you can share what you express with those who hurt you; it is a therapeutic act of detoxing your soul; the equivalent

of a nurse cleaning a wound before applying treatment.

2. ***Understand the heart of God towards you.*** God's love for you is not connected to what you do or how well you do. He loved you from before the foundations of the earth, and He loves you unconditionally. In His eyes, you are loved, valuable and worthy of the best. He is not flawed as our earthly parents are. His thoughts towards you are always good and not evil; to give you a hope and an expected end. Despite the lies you may have been fed by the enemy's schemes, choose to believe the heart of God the Father towards you. You are loved!

3. ***Seek to understand your parent's past.*** Whether you were wounded by your father, mother, or both, seek to understand their story. Very rarely does a mother or father set out to intentionally hurt their child. There is a saying I have found to be profoundly true, "Hurting people hurt people." It is possible that the way your parents raised you has a lot to do with how they were raised and even more to do with their unique life experiences. Seek to find out what their childhood was like, and seek to understand them as a person based on where they have been.

4. ***Talk to God about the pain.*** Maybe you expected this next step to be an instruction to speak with your parent if you can. Not yet. Some matters of the heart

are best dealt with at the foot of the cross first. This is the stage where you do as the Word of God instructs; pour out your heart before Him (see Psalm 62:8). One songwriter put it this way: *"Lay down the burdens of your heart; I know you'll never miss it. Show your Father where it hurts and let your Father lift it."*

5. ***Let go of the hurt.*** This may sound a bit superficial to some, but without forgiveness, true freedom is elusive. Decide to let go of the pain you have carried all these years by forgiving the one(s) who inflicted the wounds. Forgive from a place of understanding (see step 3).

Let me share a quick true story here. Karice was in her mid-thirties, and for years, she struggled with the thought that she had disappointed her father and lost his love in her teenage years because of a relationship he strongly disapproved of. She wondered why he never hugged her; she couldn't recall ever hearing him say the words, "I love you" to her. It was painful even to think about; she had a father wound.

One day, while in prayer, Karice found herself crying before God and weeping about the rejection she felt from her father. Some questions began to surface in her mind: *Why was her father so cold and aloof? Why didn't he show much emotion and was always so serious and hard to approach?* As if He were answering the questions He placed there, the Holy Spirit began to connect the dots.

Karice's Dad grew up most of his life as an orphan from the early death of his mother, then his father, to whom he was very close. He closed his heart so as never to face such hurt again. In that moment, for the first time, Karice felt compassion and empathy for her father, rather than anger and pain. She promised herself that the next time she visited her father, she would greet him with a hug instead of waiting to receive one. There began the turning point in Karice's journey to being free from the father wound and developing a relationship with her father. She had to confront her pain, bring it before her heavenly Father, and allow Him to help her see and understand her father's story and choose to let go of the pain.

1. ***Be Intentional about building a better relationship with your parent.*** This, of course, is dependent on your unique situation. Is your parent alive? Do you know where to find him or her and how to make contact? Is the parent open to improving their relationship with you? As long as the door exists, knock. Take small steps in breaking the cycle and building a better parent-child relationship than what existed before.

2. ***Don't repeat the cycle.*** If you are a parent who has experienced the effects of the mother/father wound, be intentional about not repeating the mistakes of your parent. Satan likes to work in cycles. Give him no room in your children's lives to keep the cycle of wounding going. Understand that your children are

gifts from God, and you are accountable to God for the environment in which you allow them to grow. Be present, active, loving, and engaging towards them while teaching them the way they should go.

3. ***Seek professional help if needed.*** The mother/father wound can be so engrained in your psyche that you may need the help of a trained professional counsellor or psychologist to explore, unearth and release all the toxic emotions that have thrived in the pain over the years. Don't be afraid to reach out for that kind of support, especially if after your own efforts there is little or no change in how you feel, think and behave.

4. ***Use your spiritual weapons.*** As a Kingdom citizen, you must understand that there is a spiritual warfare raging over your purpose, peace of mind, family, and destiny. When you are inflicted by a parental wound, it is no coincidence. It is a strategic ploy of the enemy of your soul to pollute and cripple you into believing you are less than who God says you are, with the intention that you will never see yourself well enough to fulfil your God-given destiny. The devil is a liar! Use your weapons of prayer, fasting, worship and the Word to fight the good fight of faith, run your race well, finish your course, and lay hold on eternal life. Be determined to rid your soul of every infectious seed planted by the enemy. Position yourself for deliverance—that place of deliverance is

in the secret place of prayer where everything is laid naked and bare before the God who will fight for you. He always causes you to triumph in Christ Jesus.

5. ***LIVE!*** Jesus said in John 10:10, *"The thief's purpose is to steal and kill and destroy. My purpose is to give them a rich and satisfying life." (NLT)*. Be determined as a child of God to be free from the offence of the mother/father wound. Release and forgive those who have hurt you, and live life out loud because of who you are in Christ. You are not what your past expected you to be. You are who God made you to be. Get connected with your heavenly Father in the secret place and be transformed into His image as you behold Him daily. Then you will be free to live and love; to live life in abundance, healed and delivered from the mother/father wounds.

In Christ we live and move and have our being.

Shalom.

Megan Y. Hylton BA, MA
Associate Counselling Psychologist
Author: Directing Your Arrows: A Strategic Approach to Successful Parenting

Chapter 9

Toxic Emotions

"Negative emotions are like unwelcome guests. Just because they show up on our doorstep doesn't mean they have a right to stay." —Deepak Chopra

Jesus emphasises that it is out of the heart evil thoughts come (see Matthew 15:19). It is therefore imperative that the heart be brought under the governance of both the scriptures and the Holy Spirit. The heart that is un-surrendered or unsubmitted to God has the potential for great harm and damage to others and yourself. The heart that has been wounded will often retaliate, even to the detriment of the individual. Many have become slaves to their own hurts. We cannot heal by continuing to hurt.

Sometimes we get caught up in harming others, notwithstanding that we are also damaging ourselves. We should never try to resolve pain by causing others to suffer in a similar way that we have. In attempting to imprison others, we have made ourselves captives. Psychological issues can affect our emotional well-being and cause us to react in a sinister way toward others.

Get rid of all bitterness, rage, anger, harsh words, and slander, as well as all types of evil behavior. Instead, be kind to each other, tenderhearted, forgiving one another, just as God through Christ has forgiven you. (Ephesians 4:31-32 - NLT).

Offence can result in a rise of toxic emotions in both the offended and the offender. This will manifest in characteristic behaviour that is harmful and driven by motive borne out of pain, anger, and retaliation.

It is possible for envy to hide in support. Jealousy can hide in compliments and hate under the presumption of love, care, and concern. What one feels can vary from what they say.

Here is a checklist for dealing with the effects of offences:

- Be considerate in dealing with others that your actions may have affected.
- Explain your actions carefully to avoid misunderstanding.
- Apologise in love for offensive actions.
- Avoid taking revenge.
- Pray for the offender and yourself.
- Accept God's grace to change.
- Understand the purpose of offence to reveal the heart.
- See offence as a natural part of life and prepare to deal with it.

- Get involved in an accountability group for support.
- Pursue peace with those without and within.
- Resolve differences speedily and do not allow it to fester.
- Love the offender/offended unconditionally.
- Seek for the restoration and reconciliation of the fallen.
- Speak the truth in love and correct from a heart of compassion.
- Approach with tenderness and firmness.
- Listen to them and offer Spirit-led advice.
- Give them an opportunity to heal.
- Work with and not against.

Toxic behaviour is often exemplified by highly insecure people. This makes them extremely difficult to deal with, and often puts a strain on interpersonal relationships. In some cases, they attempt to conceal the behaviour or simply compensate for their self-doubt. They can be averse to taking risks and be highly unproductive. They can also display a level of aggression that is reflected in being nasty or abusive.

The following are a list of common toxic behaviours according to Amy Gallo:

1. They are overly concerned about what others think about them.
2. They never express a firm opinion.

3. They suffer from a chronic ability to make decisions, even when the choices have little consequence.
4. They frequently try to change the direction of projects and meetings.
5. They put other people down to make themselves look more important.
6. They constantly talk about how busy they are (when they are not) to show that they are in demand.
7. They are paranoid meddlers who make you question your every move.

How to deal with insecure people:

1. **Evaluate the magnitude of the problem**—this can be done through counting the number of negative and positive interactions you have had with them.
2. **Identify what triggers the problem**—try to determine, during your interactions, what causes the negative reactions to surface.
3. **Demonstrate genuine compassion**—having their best interest at heart coupled with a heart of empathy could help tremendously in bridging the gap.
4. **Face to face moments**—these are casual one-on-one interactions that allow for you to know the person more.
5. **Work towards a positive outcome**—the general focus here is on creating the type of interaction that will add value to the individual by allowing them to overcome the insecurities.

6. **Be clear in your communication**—ensure that the communication flows, leaving no room for doubt or ambiguity.
7. **Work together**—allow for greater security during the discussions through facilitating a strong sense of ownership by them.
8. **Have a steady plan for progress**—don't allow them to be overwhelmed by involvement in too many activities. Allow for a steady pace with periodic evaluation.
9. **Show that you are not a threat**—they need to see you as an ally and not a rival. Show gratitude and appreciation coupled with complements that would indicate that progress is being made. This will help to boost self-confidence.

The Cancel Culture And Offence

Cancel Culture primarily involves people joining in to take a public stand against an individual, usually a public figure or groups, for actions considered offensive, for bad behaviour and, in most cases, without a chance for redemption as a means to deter similar actions in the future. It has been described as counterproductive in fuelling hostile behaviour and jeopardising professional careers.

It has been called a negative, even toxic, way of simplifying complex issues and encouraging snap judgments that can easily result in overly harsh consequences in less offensive situations (Steven A. Hassan).

The practice is representative of the current cultural climate, which is heavily influenced by the digital world people have become accustomed to so much that there is no distinction between public and private.

- The cancel culture encourages shame not accountability, focusing on the individuals and failing to acknowledge the systemic issues that are at the root of hateful behaviour.
- It can be more entertainment than accountability.
- Doesn't just affect the cancelled and the cancellers; it can wreak havoc on the mental health of onlookers.
- Causes guilt for those with convictions that are afraid to speak out against what they deem an injustice.
- Causes worry and anxiety that others will find something in their past to use against them.
- Results in the boycotting or removal of support from someone based on what they have said verbally or in writing.
- Apart from the invasion of privacy, it can put you physically at risk.
- Creates online censorship on public discourses, thereby stifling free speech and the exchange of ideas.
- Can cause job loss and result in an identity crisis.
- Fears that everything you say or write will be examined microscopically and construed as offensive, even if it was not meant to be.

- Affects one's freedom of expression as some may fall silent, not feeling comfortable sharing their thoughts on any given matter.
- Being cancelled can lead to teen anxiety, depression, trauma and suicidal thoughts and behaviour.
- For teens, it can cause social ostracization at an age when peer connections are vitally important.
- Causes persons to become disagreeable simply because they disagree with you.

How to protect your mental health against cancel culture:

- **Avoid posting when your emotions are heightened**— if someone pushes your trigger, don't rush to your keyboard but take some time to calm down. Remember, internet users may never forget what you wrote, and it may leave an indelible imprint on people's minds.
- **Have others review your post first**—we may not recognise the effects of our own words. What we may deem initially to be acceptably might, after scrutiny, be seen as offensive and overtly aggressive. Someone reviewing what is to be posted can bring to light potential issues that could inadvertently hurt someone.
- **If you were wrong, then apologise**—craft a genuine and well thought through response and share it when ready. Even though it may not be accepted by all, it will soften the views that some may have of you and

reduce their desire to make you public enemy number one.

- **Try to see the other side**—rather than immediately retaliate, understand how your words may have affected or offended others. This can influence further communication and keep you from potentially making the same mistakes.
- **Take a break from social media**—cutting back on posts and outbursts is a way of improving your mental health and avoiding many toxic situations. This could reduce both depression and loneliness from being attacked and side-lined.
- **Talk to someone**—it is important to reach out to someone you trust or a professional to help you recover.

Recognise also that individuals come from different backgrounds, experiences and beliefs that may differ from yours, and they may not see eye to eye with you on various issues. Awareness can stop you from doing or saying something that can make you become an unintentional target. You don't have to intend to offend for your actions to be deemed offensive. The damage is done once the offence is perceived or received. Learning from your experience can make you become stronger and wiser in the use of public spaces and forums.

Whereas some aspects of cancel culture can be useful in holding people accountable for bad behaviour, there are other aspects that are akin to cyberbullying that can be damaging. Overcoming may require you to recognise that the rejection and ostracization being experienced does not define who you are as a person.

Dealing With The Toxic Effects Of Bitterness

"Bitterness is unforgiveness fermented." —Gregory Popcak

Look after each other so that none of you fails to receive the grace of God. Watch out that no poisonous root of bitterness grows up to trouble you, corrupting many. (Hebrews 12:15 - NLT).

When bitterness is allowed to develop within the heart, it both corrupts and defiles the individual. Bitterness and genuine gratitude to God cannot co-exist. Bitterness normally springs from unhealed hurts caused intentionally or unintentionally. Feeling bitter is typically a consequence of accumulated anger and sadness because of past experiences in life, which resulted in losses or disappointments. The bitter person normally feels that life has let them down due to ill-defined forces working against them despite their best efforts.

Bitterness not only causes signs of trauma like sleepiness, fatigue, and lack of libido, but it can also, in the long-term, lead to low self-confidence, negative personality shifts, and an inability to have a healthy relationship. Bitterness results in an unwillingness to let go of offences and disappointments but instead being focussed on seeking revenge for the hurts experienced.

Unforgiveness, if untreated, will ultimately lead to bitterness. A person who is bitter will not reason objectively and, most times, will justify their actions and behaviour as the reasonable thing to do. When bitterness remains unresolved, it tends to affect all relationships and influence the perception we have of others and how we are viewed and treated by them. We tend to view others through the lenses of our own pains, discomforts, and disappointments and that may cause us to withdraw, isolating ourselves from the company and fellowship with others. It can cause us to be cold, biased, discriminating, distant and abrupt and condescending when dealing with the warmth exuded by others. Our discomfort and emotional baggage result in too high a cost for relationship maintenance from others and further burdens us with thoughts of rejection and ostracization.

Bitterness can cause us to feel unloved, pessimistic, and emotionally distanced from others, drowning in the sea of despondency and despair, and may ultimately lead to depression.

What Causes Bitterness?

- Traumatic childhood experiences.
- Feelings of abandonment by friends and loved ones.
- Repetitive failures and disappointments.

- Financial downfall.
- Bad career moves.
- Loss of possession or loved ones.
- Abused and misused by others.
- Chronic health issues.
- Constantly being compared to others.
- Feelings of inadequacy.

Characteristics Of Bitterness

- Unwillingness to let go of grudges (unforgiving) like their life depended on it.
- Quick to blame others for their own disappointments and problems.
- Harbouring evil thoughts towards anyone who has hurt them.
- Unwillingness to share in another person's joy or successes (jealous).
- Lack of gratitude or appreciation for the good experienced in life.
- Constantly focus on the negative aspects of life.
- Obsessive thoughts of revenge.
- Suspicious and cynical of life and people.
- Resentment.
- Highly critical and judgmental.
- Feeling misunderstood and undervalued.
- Tend to be narcissistic (everything is always about them and their emotions).

- Constantly irritated and bothered by even the simplest of things.
- Controlling and aggressive in relationships.

Characteristics Of A Bitter Person

- A bitter person finds it impossible to speak amicably with others within family or in other interpersonal relationships. The emotional pain experienced causes them to lash out at anyone trying to help them. This becomes their primary defense mechanism.
- A bitter person speaks with harsh words that cut and wound others deeply. Words are used as a weapon to disguise the inner pain felt. The effect is to make others feel hurt because they themselves are hurting. If they are not happy, then no one else deserves to be happy either.
- A bitter person uses language characterized by hostility and suspicion. This is for a sense of control that does not help them. They have emotional guard dogs constantly on duty.
- A bitter person points out other's faults because it takes the attention off their own shortcomings.
- A bitter person appears to be disrespectful to others and is unthankful. It is evident in their displays of ingratitude. They reason that showing gratitude is to reveal they had a need, and since they had a need, that means they are weak, and if they are weak, then that makes them vulnerable, and if they are

vulnerable, they can get hurt, and if they get hurt, they have to show pain.

- A bitter person rehearses/ruminates over the past repeatedly. This causes the person to feel the pain repeatedly and, as such, build up and display venomous attitudes. They are not free; they are locked to the past.
- A bitter person seems to have a vendetta against others that causes them to pull everyone down to their level.

How To Deal With Bitterness

- Acknowledge your emotions about the harm done to you, recognizing how those emotions affect your behaviour, and work to release them.
- Choose to forgive the person who offended you despite the pain and anguish felt.
- Release the control and power that the offending person and situation have had on your life.
- Resist the temptation of constantly keeping up to date with the life and activities of the person who has triggered the feelings of resentment and hurt that you now harbour.
- Be willing to accept the support and help from well-intentioned individuals who want to facilitate your health and recovery. It may also be necessary to recruit the services of a trained professional.

- Be optimistic that change is not only possible, but also inevitable. This change however will require hard work and dedication to the task at hand.
- **Journal.** When the pain comes, write down the emotions that come with the pain. Writing will help lessen the pain and help to put your thoughts into better perspective. However, please do not use this tool to write down how you are going to take revenge on the person. As you journal, seek God's perspectives and healing regarding the situation.
- **Make a conscious effort to forgive.** Be mindful that forgiveness is a decision. Avoid thinking that the size of the offence does not merit quickly forgiving the offender. Each offended person may take a different duration in time to both process and deal with the offence. The deeper the pain, the longer it may take to forgive. The important thing however is to initiate the process of dealing with the hurt. As you forgive, you may not lose the memory of the events that led to the bitterness, but you will feel less resentful towards the offender until eventually you feel no pain or hurt.
- **Look at God's grace toward us.** At the root of our Christian faith is grace. We were at enmity with God, and He gave us grace through His Son, Jesus Christ. This grace will empower us to extend forgiveness to others who have hurt us even as we have received forgiveness and reconciliation from God. Because we have become beneficiaries of God's grace, the expectation is that we should always extend it to

those who have hurt us (See Ephesians 2:8, Colossians 3:13).

Toxic emotions must be identified, and the appropriate remedy and treatment applied. The longer it remains unattended, the more difficult (but not impossible) it is to treat. It is important that we allow the appropriate time for healing and recovery once the treatment begins.

Chapter 10

Wounding With Intent

"It is just as much an offence to take offence as it is to give offence." —Ken Kesey

And if someone asks, 'Then what about those wounds on your chest?' he will say, 'I was wounded at my friends' house!' (Zechariah 13:6 - NLT).

This prophecy by Zechariah speaks to the coming Messiah, Jesus, being wounded in the house of His friends. Jesus was wounded because of His assignment (transgression and iniquities). Offence results in deep-seated wounds. He was rejected by the very race that He came to bring redemption to. The betrayal of Christ was painful but intentional in terms of the purpose it fulfilled. His betrayal was important in both His glorification and propitiation for our sins. Jesus never became bitter though He suffered at the hands of His enemies. He was able to look beyond the abuse and see the hand of God at work for good out of an evil situation.

He did not retaliate when he was insulted, nor threaten revenge when he suffered. He left his case in the hands of God, who always judges fairly. (1 Peter 2:23 - NLT).

Ministry is often birthed through being wounded. The wounds seem to be the price one pays to develop an appreciation and identification for the sufferings of others. This empathy can lead to compassion and compassion to ministry. Wounds result in pain and guilt. It exposes you to intense and heartfelt suffering. Wounds may be severe but not mortal. It may be constantly reopened through our interactions with others, but they may become both a defining and a teachable moment. Sword represents the word that comes from your mouth, which can have a piercing effect on others.

Wounds should not prevent you from providing hope and healing to others, neither should being under duress result in despair or frustration. There is a difference between a bruise and a wound. A wound causes quick damage—the skin tissue is cut or punctured while a bruise (also called a closed wound) is where the skin is not torn. A wound is usually caused by a sharp object, but bruises are the result of blunt force or trauma. A wound almost certainly bleeds due to ruptured tissue and blood vessels. Betrayal of trust can cause significant damage where the external signs might belie the internal pain.

The wounds caused by offence can drive one to the fulfilment of purpose. It can become that signal for introspection that later rallies us into the direction that God is calling us into.

Offence can make one bitter not better.

An open rebuke is better than hidden love! *Wounds from a sincere friend are better than many kisses from an enemy. (Proverbs 27:5-6 - NLT).*

Open rebuke refers to confronting someone's misbehaviour frankly and truthfully. Its receptivity might be based on perception, especially if it is harsh or exposes a behaviour that the preference would be for it to remain hidden. Even though it may cause offence, we are reminded to speak the truth in love. The rebuke may hurt the friend's ego but, if given and taken in the spirit of love, will aid the delinquent brother in his development and maturity. There are not many people who will embrace friends who can identify their faults and who will courageously speak their mind about them because they care. The normal tendency is to seek friends who are weak morally, that we can control, and lord it over, who will never see anything wrong with anything we do and will follow us right over the cliff. Most people want friends who are always in agreement with their decisions. We don't want people of integrity who will tell us the ugly truth about ourselves, whose words will cut us deep, hurt our feelings, and whose rebuke our conscience agrees with even if we try to stifle it.

Then we will no longer be immature like children. We won't be tossed and blown about by every wind of new teaching. We will not be influenced when people try to trick us with lies so clever they sound like the truth. Instead, we will speak the truth in love, growing in every way more and more like Christ, who is the head of his body, the church. (Ephesians 4:14-15 - NLT).

Sometimes care and concern over the welfare of others can result in the kind of rebuke that will hurt but is intended to promote health. The real mark of a true friend is that they will wound us with loving correction. Sometimes you will hurt before you heal. The wounds are a metaphor for the painful and plain words that must be spoken to heal and cause the restoration of relationships. This is opposed to the deceit by an enemy appearing to offer a friendly gesture.

The Word of God will be used to both encourage and rebuke so the person can begin to walk in honour. You will not coddle, compromise, or overlook actions that hurt their relationship with God or lead them into sinful habits and practices. Hatred is behind lying words. You can't desire the best for someone and lie to them about what could be detrimental.

Wounding with intent exemplifies the theme of tough love where offending is unavoidable, but it does not serve the ulterior motive of pulling down or causing one to stumble but rather to correct a particular behaviour or action. It is therefore intended to offer correction with the view to dealing with a negative behaviour.

It is important that we discern that not all offending situations are destined for our demise or downfall. Some are well intentioned to foster spiritual growth and development. David recognised the importance of correction coming from those who cared, even though it may wound, or cause hurt.

Let the godly strike me! It will be a kindness! If they correct me, it is soothing medicine. Don't let me refuse it. But I pray constantly against the wicked and their deeds. (Psalm 141:5 - NLT).

With wisdom there is a willingness to accept correction and apply oneself for life change no matter how sharp the words may be. To ignore correction is to fall into the trap of self-deception and disillusionment. Those who need to be helped, even if offended by the rebuke, will see its value, and make a change for the better rather than descending into bitterness.

The correction of the righteous, even if it offends, is seen as kindness based on its restorative value. The correction is well intentioned and not done out of malice or anger. It may initially hit hard but has the potential to help avert potential disaster. Like medicine, the correction can only take effect when it is administered and embraced. It is important to be both open and humble than waste or refuse such a valuable resource.

So don't bother correcting mockers; they will only hate you. But correct the wise, and they will love you. (Proverbs 9:8 - NLT).

The truth should never be stated from a self-righteous and arrogant position. We must always remember that the motive is to correct to improve and not to condemn and drive away. Even when the offence might lead to resistance, we must never allow ourselves to be offended by those we are trying to correct.

But Peter took him aside and began to reprimand him for saying such things. "Heaven forbid, Lord," he said. "This will never happen to you!" Jesus turned to Peter and said, "Get away from me, Satan! You are a dangerous trap to me. You are seeing things merely from a human point of view, not from God's." (Matthew 16:22-23 – NLT).

What Jesus said deeply offended Peter who refused to accept that this could have been the destiny of the Messiah he followed. Sometimes offence comes because of ignorance to the truth. To Peter, who was looking for a militant leader to overthrow roman domination and to restore Israel, this was not what he had signed up for, and demanded that Jesus withdraw His remarks.

Peter was obviously wounded, and his belief system took a battering. Jesus recognised that the perception of Peter was not in sync with divine will and destiny and so addressed the real perpetrator of this anti-redemption philosophy. The rebuke was intended to realign Peter's thinking and provide correction. We should always be open to seeing things from God's point of view.

Gently instruct those who oppose the truth. Perhaps God will change those people's hearts, and they will learn the truth. (2 Timothy 2:25 - NLT).

Having spoken the word to correct, we must leave room for the Holy Spirit to operate by bringing conviction which, when heeded, will lead to life change.

The wounds of a friend are like prescription medicine that once administered will help the wounded to recover and be nursed back to a state of good health. Healing requires obedience to the prescription extended for complete restoration to take place.

The human spirit can endure a sick body, but who can bear a crushed spirit? (Proverbs 18:14 - NLT).

Those who sin should be reprimanded in front of the whole church; this will serve as a strong warning to others. (1 Timothy 5:20 - NLT).

Sins in this context are considered to be evil actions committed publicly and have become common knowledge in the community, having fallen into the public domain, and must therefore be addressed publicly within the church. This will discourage others from being emboldened to fall into the same pattern of misconduct. The rebuke is meant to expose the deviant behaviour and to offer correction thereby causing a change in behaviour. Open rebuke is not meant for humiliation but rather reconciliation and the development of a healthy reverence for God and His standards of right. This is expected to cause us to deal with the misgivings in our own lives, and for others not to venture into the practices highlighted.

Chapter 11

Self-Care and Emotional Well-Being From Offence

"Every one of us needs to show how much we care for each other and, in the process, care for ourselves." —Princess Diana

What is self-care? There are common misconceptions concerning what self-care means or looks like, including but not limited to the myth that it is synonymous with self-indulgence and selfishness. Be it far from it, self-care is being empowered in taking care of our overall well-being so we can be healthy and show up for ourselves and others in any or all eight areas: physical, psychological, emotional, social, professional, environmental, spiritual, and financial.

No doubt, in today's culture, propelled on all social media platforms, is what some view as the over-sensationalized trend of self-care. A quick glance on Instagram often shows influencers, content creators and the average person using the trending hashtag #selfcare with a photo or video highlighting a spa day, manicures and pedicures, a luxury retreat or a mug filled with tea, a bottle of champagne or a glass of wine. Consider a leisurely stroll as well on the beach, nature walk, silent solace, and breathing routines. Let's not dismiss the curated behaviour and mental health resources and therapy. While these gross oversimplifications of the concept of self-care and indulgences are great, serving many different purposes, one aspect of self-care and emotional well-being that is often overlooked and many individuals struggle with stems from offence, especially within Christian culture.

Whether the offence was an intentional or unintended slight misinterpretation, a rejection, insult, or any form of verbal and emotional abuse, they are all issues of hurt feelings. Unfaced, unresolved hurts have the potential to be destructive. It can spread like an uncontrolled California wildfire with flames of bitterness, anger and unforgiveness that eventually spreads into our hearts and creates steel barricades. Left untreated, it becomes difficult to let go. The effects are evident in the breakdown and disruption of our interpersonal relationships: family, friendships, acquaintances, romantic, professional, and our relationship with God.

A brother offended is harder to be won than a strong city: and their connections are like the bars of a castle. (Proverbs 18:19 - KJV).

Now let me briefly address the elephant in the room. One of the biggest controversies of late is the taboo and negative connotation among religious leaders concerning the "Self-Help" industry. The questions posed are "Should Christians read self-help books? Is there a place in a Christian life for self-care, self-worth, and self-love? Should one have self-worth or is that the same as being prideful? Instead of answering these questions or giving my opinion, I pray that you will approach this with Godly discernment and interpretation of context, so I will pose this question to you: Be it resolved that the Bible cannot contradict itself; Does the Bible admonish us to devalue and hate ourselves?

Offence has its impact on self-worth. Undoubtably, we have all been wounded by some form of offence: threatening behaviours, hurtful words, actions, gestures, even degrading looks.

Offences through words possess immense power to be life-threatening and can annihilate dreams, visions and hopes.

Death and life are in the power of the tongue: and they that love it shall eat the fruit thereof. (Proverbs 18:21 - KJV).

These experiences can inflict intense pain and hold us in a space that is painfully turbulent. This blow of honour to our person triggers self-conscious emotions and rips the umbrella of humiliation, exposing pride, shame, and guilt.

Let no corrupt communication proceed out of your mouth, but that which is good to the use of edifying, that it may minister grace unto the hearers. (Ephesians 4:29 - KJV).

The attack is perceived as the offender's evaluation of you. Your integrity is tossed around, and negative self-perceptions develop because of the offence. The wound often leaves you feeling invisible, insignificant, and devalued.

Reproach hath broken my heart; and I am full of heaviness: and I looked for some to take pity, but there was none; and for comforters, but I found none. (Psalm 69:20 - KJV).

The danger of offence is the distorted messages of worth. Worth is a translation of the Greek word *axios*, which means "of weight and worth." When we look at the concept of worth, it basically signifies the value of a person or a thing. In terms of self-worth, it is akin to the belief of value and significance.

Journey with me in your mind to an auction, or maybe you can remember movie scenes of an auction where folks gathered and, at the end of the day, paid crazy money for items that to us on the outside may seem insignificant, overpriced, and of no worth or value. The reality is, at any auction, the worth of an item is determined by the highest price. May I remind you, that despite the emotional upheaval and mayhem you have been through from an offence, whether your scars are visible or not, you are valuable and worth it all. Over 2000 years ago—the highest price—the bid was paid for you. When God sent His Son, Jesus Christ, as the ultimate sacrifice, though not yet born, you and I, our worth, value and significance were displayed and established forever.

Now, let's be honest; it is disheartening when people minimize the importance of your emotions, when in essence, the offence wounds your spirit. It can consume your thoughts and impede emotional growth and your ability to live your God-given purpose. The unresolved offence can affect your ability to carry out daily routine tasks and become the driving force behind your choices. Thoughts influence choices, and choices shape behaviours, behaviours create the experience, experience stimulates emotions, and emotions rebirth thoughts. Everything begins and is released in the atmosphere from your thoughts.

The spirit of a man will sustain his infirmity; but a wounded spirit who can bear? (Proverbs 18:14 - KJV).

Listen, a self-worth struggler dealing with an offence is a real deal. In 2 Samuel 9, Mephibosheth, Jonathan's son, crippled in both feet and unable to stand or engage in battle, struggled with self-worth. In today's society, he would have been subject somewhat to the "cancel culture' experience. Coming from such a high royal chain, the grandson of King Saul, despite his royal bloodline, battled drowning experiences of financial and emotional times, which eventually sucked him into a quicksand of unsustainability.

He found himself living in Lo-Debar, which means "House of No Bread." When he was summoned to appear before King David with a mindset that his life had no value, he shuffled his lame feet and threw himself before the king and declared himself a "dead dog." David's response astonished him:

And David said unto him, Fear not: for I will surely shew thee kindness for Jonathan thy father's sake, and will restore thee all the land of Saul thy father; and thou shalt eat bread at my table continually." (2 Samuel 9:7 - KJV).

Kindness and compassion were extended unto him despite the offence and murderous vengeance streak of King Saul, his grandfather. David's covenant with Johnathan was extended to Mephibosheth.

Then said Ziba unto the king, According to all that my lord the king hath commanded his servant, so shall thy servant do. As for Mephibosheth, said the king, he shall eat at my table, as one of the king's sons. (2 Samuel 9:11 - KJV).

His physical conditions did not change; he still shuffled to the table and around the palace. However, what he once felt—low self-worth and worthlessness—was restored to infinite worth and value as a result of the king's grace.

If you are presently suffering from an offence that has crippled your emotions, self-worth, value and have you feeling a sense of inferiority, may I remind you that the King of kings has extended His grace, kindness and compassion to you. Your scars and physical appearance may be evident to others, but shuffle your way to the table. You have been adopted into His family, and you have immeasurable worth.

According as he hath chosen us in him before the foundation of the world, that we should be holy and without blame before him in love: Having predestined us unto the adoption of children by Jesus Christ to himself, according to the good pleasure of his will," (Ephesians 1:4-5 - KJV).

Checklist Of Low Self-Worth

Do an honest inventory of where you are in the emotional sphere. Place a checkmark at the questions below that are true to you.

Do you struggle with inner insecurities?
☐ Yes ☐ No

Do you say negative things about yourself?
☐ Yes ☐ No

Do you repeat negative words that others say about you?
☐ Yes ☐ No

Are you unhappy with your personal achievements?
☐ Yes ☐ No

Do you struggle with comparison?

☐ Yes ☐ No

Do you struggle with rejection?

☐ Yes ☐ No

Do you self-hate and engage in negative behaviour to alleviate the pain?

☐ Yes ☐ No

Are you negligent of your appearance?

☐ Yes ☐ No

Do you struggle with unforgiveness?

☐ Yes ☐ No

Do you look for the approval of others?

☐ Yes ☐ No

Do you struggle with an unfaced, untreated offence?

☐ Yes ☐ No

Do you struggle with accepting compliments?

☐ Yes ☐ No

Do you struggle with defending yourself?

☐ Yes ☐ No

Are you reluctant to express your true feelings due to an offence?

☐ Yes ☐ No

Self-Worth Substitute Checklist

More often, when one struggles with self-worth, there is an attempt to make up with an emotional deficit. Use the checklist below to honestly see where you are.

Do you crave or find yourself constantly striving for recognition?

☐ Yes ☐ No

Do you struggle with an addiction to substances, sex, food shopping and gambling.

☐ Yes ☐ No

Do you live a fake, lavish life, financially extravagant to impress others?

☐ Yes ☐ No

Do you hang your basket out of reach? Are you impressed with status beyond your financial capabilities?

☐ Yes ☐ No

Are you overly competitive?

☐ Yes ☐ No

The Haemorrhage Of Untreated Offence

I am a firm believer of the benefits of shared stories. My opening quote for my podcast and the theme throughout is:

"There is therapeutic value in shared stories, but knowing when to share, why we share, and to whom we share with, is vitally important." —Denise Hinkson Lawrence.

In a culture where transparency is the evidence that people are looking for to speak to one's credibility, many are unmasking and that, in itself, is a good thing but also has its drawbacks. Many of us live with the thought that "our" struggles are just that— "ours"—and no one else is or have experienced what we have or are currently dealing with. This, sometimes, if we are not careful, will put us in a victim mentality mindset.

Now when we see and hear others, be it a celebrity or someone of status that we can connect with, unmask their pains, struggles and setbacks, we are either blown away with shock or we are empowered and encouraged to know that we are not alone. Knowing that others have been there, done that and are wearing the t-shirt fuels the drive to self-care and emotional well-being of offences. Speaking of emotional well-being, this, in a nutshell, is the demonstration of our ability to process and navigate our emotions in coping with life's challenges and difficulties. How we manage stress, pain, and offences has an effect on our mental health. Some of us are able to foster positive social connections, others are unable to handle the shipwreck of the offences, and our trauma leads to unrighteous anger, which eventually enslaves us. Unfortunately, we have seen and heard far too many, including religious leaders and notable individuals, who are hurt or have experienced hurt, struggling with unresolved resentment, offences, and overwhelming emotions spiralling out of control, and they speak, coach, preach, teach and produce digital and printed materials of bitterness. Listen, the evidence that you are not healed is when you share your story and there is no evidence of God's grace; nothing that can be attributed to His involvement in your healing journey. There is no testimony of how He delivered you, through His Word, therapy, counselling, prayer, conferences, workshops, or training opportunities. This then results in divisions among family members, professional environment, religious organizations, visceral pain, and a secular world with more ammunition in their hands to bash Christianity.

"Pain is inevitable. Suffering is optional." —Unknown

"...knowing when to share, why we share and with whom we share is vitally important." —Denise Hinkson Lawrence

When we share from a hurt or an unresolved space or an unhealed perspective, we then haemorrhage unto others. The bleeding is now stained on people who were not the offenders, and innocent people are now paying the penalties and consequences of your unresolved offence, pain, and struggles. We destroy relationships and so many lives when we transfer aggression, anger, and bitterness to others. Poor practice of communication can destroy lives.

What I have learned is ,that pain is non-discriminatory. It is blinded to race, financial status, education and other achievements and accomplishments. Pain is nonbiased to gender, agnostic, non-denominational, atheist or Christian. It is a part of life; the unwelcomed guests. It is how we cope with the pain, the inseparable offence that we somehow cannot seem to divorce that speaks volume. For sure, the emotional baggage can become lighter when you engage in some aspect of emotional well-being; therapy, Christian counselling, and self-help strategies. It is vital that we make every effort to ensure that we thoroughly deal with our previous hurts, pain, and offences. If not, anyone who comes in contact with us will become a victim of our "unhealed" hurt.

Let's practice accountability. Avoid immature opportunities to speak, share, write, teach or preach and participate in engagements that will allow you to wound others in an effort to heal yourself. Do me a favour, better yet, do yourself a favour; get healed before you enter a new relationship, business venture, leadership role or position of influence. There are many options, strategies, and techniques available to you and, at the end of the day, how you feel can affect your ability to be who God has called and purpose you to be, so take care of your emotional well-being so you can show up being true to yourself and others.

Face your offences, struggles and pain. Don't bottle them in; forgive yourself and the offenders. Unforgiveness is like boiling a pot of oil with the intent of throwing it at your offender and the wind blows it back on you. Sounds intense, I know, but it is the reality. Forgiveness is part of your healing; let go and grow. The myth is that when you forgive the offender, he or she is getting off the hook, or that we will forget the offence. Listen, the key thing you need to focus on is that when you forgive, the grace of God will allow the stings of the offence to fade. The actual event, offence, pain, or situation may not be erased from your memory, but the effect of the sting of it can be alleviated through God's power.

Continue to live and you will see that life is an endless cycle of resentment and retaliation, and ups and downs. Be intentional to grow through your hurt, offences, and pain.

Like everyone, I have experienced hurt profoundly as well as trivial instances. However, what I have learned in my journey of emotional well-being is that it is a part of the process. I remind myself every day with a personal quote:

"Pain is not happening to me, but for me, to pull me to the place where God's purpose will have me." —Denise Hinkson Lawrence

Forgiveness is always possible. Alexander Pope says, *"to err is human, but to forgive is divine."* Forgiveness must come from your heart, the core of your being. It is the only space where your mind and emotions come together. Be intentional and committed to your well-being and be emotionally vulnerable before God—it is the key to you becoming emotionally free.

And we know that all things work together for good to them that love God, to them who are the called according to his purpose. (Romans 8:28 - KJV).

Rev. Denise Hinkson Lawrence

Owner of Women 2 Women LLC

Life Coach, Author, Podcaster, Speaker and Host

Conclusion

The greatest of truth is only beneficial when the concepts are applied resulting in the evidence of a transformed life. It is the hope and expectation of the author that there will be a deliberate attempt to allow the words to affirm in some and influence in others the importance of dealing with offence, the offender and the offended.

Dealing with offence is often described as a work in progress. Whichever side of the discussion we sit on, the need for appropriate action is deemed necessary. There is the admission that many of the issues raised, and the solutions provided will take time and commitment before there is evidence of transformation. A more reasoned approach to problem-solving is required.

The main thrust cannot just be identifying what is wrong in others but also what needs to be corrected in us.

We tend to give what we have received. What has been stored or bottled up is often delivered to the undeserving. We find an outlet for release on the unsuspecting because we are afraid to retaliate in kind on those who have caused us harm, hurt or injury. It becomes easy to hit out even on those who have been trying to help.

Sometimes those offended might throw themselves into work and other activities to self-medicate against offences. This only puts off the inevitable because the problem remains unresolved. Withdrawal to activities that takes your mind off conflict does not resolve the issues at hand. Insecurities caused by offence can be a challenge to peace and harmony in communications.

Whereas we can identify both the cause and characteristics of offence, it is important that we move on to the curative aspects of it. This volume provides a recipe for dealing with oneself, whether you are the perpetrator or the victim.

Other Books by the Author

Made in the USA
Columbia, SC
07 November 2024

5fca89f4-5b20-4494-87d9-34f79e7d0c36R03